D1263270

Angel Crafts

Graceful Gifts and Inspired Designs for 47 Projects

Holly Harrison

GLOUCESTER MASSACHUSETTS

ROCKPORT PUBLISHERS

© 2002 by Rockport Publishers, Inc.

All rights reserved. No part of this book may be reproduced in any form without written permission of the copyright owners. All images in this book have been reproduced with the knowledge and prior consent of the artists concerned and no responsibility is accepted by producer, publisher, or printer for any infringement of copyright or otherwise, arising from the contents of this publication. Every effort has been made to ensure that credits accurately comply with information supplied.

First published in the United States of America by
Rockport Publishers, Inc.
33 Commercial Street
Gloucester, Massachusetts 01930-5089
Telephone: (978) 282-9590
Fax: (978) 283-2742
www.rockpub.com

ISBN 1-56496-852-9
10 9 8 7 6 5 4 3 2 1

Cover and Book Design: Susan Raymond
Photography: Bobbie Bush Photography
Project Manager: Candie Frankel
Proofreader: Kathleen Berlew
Pattern Art: Lorraine Dey Studio

Printed in China

Introduction

You can learn to talk with them if you watch *Oprah*. You might see them dressed as Elvis loving you tender from the wall of a funky downtown café. They even have their own prime-time television shows. In fact, angels are more popular now than they were during their medieval heyday, when philosophers puzzled over how many could dance on the head of a pin. The good news is, you don't need an advanced degree to appreciate them. You might see them as spirits of faith and healing; you might get a kick out of folk-art icons such as flying haloed dogs or winged Latin saints; or you might just like making angelic dolls as gifts for the special people in your life.

Angel Crafts: Graceful Gifts and Inspired Designs for 47 Projects honors the spirit of angels in all their forms, while also looking to expand the definition of "folk" in folk art to be as inclusive as possible.

In these pages, you'll find a classical Greek-like beauty whose flowing robes of polymer clay shine like hand-hammered gold; real woman angels who show off curvy figures in glittery flapper dresses; a Latina angel in a white corn husk gown sparkling with silver stars; Thai angels wearing traditional Hill Tribe garb; an African-American angel with wide, protective wings and a colorful headdress; and a pale muslin angel demurely wearing a tea-dyed muslin dress and sporting shaggy, muslin-strip hair.

In the making of this book, I have worked with some artists who specialize in angels and others who gamely decided to apply their expertise in a particular medium to making an angel for the first time. Their creativity, their whimsical or serious natures, and their ability to envision angels in myriad ways will, I hope, inspire you through the many remarkable designs that are included here.

—Holly Harrison

GENERAL CRAFT AND SEWING SUPPLIES

In addition to the materials specified for each project, you'll need to have the following general craft and sewing supplies and household items on hand.

• Craft supplies include scissors, a craft knife and self-healing cutting mat, a metal ruler, a pencil and a fine-tip permanent black marker, low-tack masking tape, fine- and medium-grit sandpaper, artist's and foam paintbrushes in assorted sizes, tracing and transfer papers, template plastic, bristol board, and spray adhesive.

• Sewing supplies include thread to match your fabrics plus black and white, dressmaker shears, straight pins, a tape measure, an air-soluble marking pen, an iron and ironing board, hand-sewing needles, and a seam ripper. The project materials list will specify whether a sewing machine is required.

• Common household items include rubbing alcohol and cotton balls, tweezers, measuring cups, spray glass cleaner, and paper towels. It's assumed you'll have access to basic household appliances such as an oven, refrigerator, kitchen timer, washing machine, and dryer.

Patterns for the projects are printed on the project page itself or in the pattern section beginning on page 114. The light blue patterns on the project pages are actual-size and can be traced directly from the book. More information about using the patterns, including how to make templates, can be found on page 114.

Although artists' portrayals of angels have evolved through the ages, the traditional ideal has been that of an elegant, winged creature in a long, flowing gown living amid the clouds or hovering over some sort of mystical burning plant life. The angels you'll find in *Angel Crafts* are a little more down-to-earth than this.

Using materials such as joint compound, common kitchen spices, colorful fabrics, recycled metals, satin ribbons, and various found objects, the artists whose works appear in this first chapter have all taken humble everyday objects and turned them into inspired creations that range from quirky to elegant, playful to pious, hands-off to user-friendly.

Close to Home

From the angel whose halo is a silver-plated sugar spoon to the African-American angel made of quilted fabrics to the Amazon warrior whose regal gown is a simple corn husk painted white and sprinkled with silver stars, this is a group that is "media savvy" as well as culturally diverse.

And while each angel is a unique representation of its maker's vision, they all share a sense of warm domesticity, a sense that here are angels who, when properly treated and appreciated, will turn even a house that seems ordinary into a much-loved home.

Hang this trio of charming cherubs in the entry hall or above a doorway and let them welcome guests to your home. Easy-to-master techniques for applying joint compound and crackle medium to a plywood surface give them the look of age-old plaster, while their radiant baby faces shine blessings on all who walk by.

Artist: Kelly A. Henderson

Welcoming Cherubim

MATERIALS
FOR THREE CHERUBIM TILES

• three 3½" to 5" (9 cm to 13 cm) plastic cherubs

• three 8½" x 8½" x ¾" (22 cm x 22 cm x 2 cm) plywood tiles

• 1 quart (1 liter) all-purpose joint compound

• crackle medium

• acrylic paints in white, cream, and medium aqua-green

• matte acrylic spray sealer

• craft glue

• cake-decorating supplies: disposable bag, coupler, tip #61

• butter knife

• general craft supplies

1. Preheat the oven to 190°F (88°C). Glue a cherub to each plywood tile. Using a butter knife, apply joint compound around the cherubs and over the tiles. Do not make the surface look smooth, but "frost" it like a cake.

2. Attach the tip and coupler to a cake-decorating bag, and fill the bag halfway with joint compound. On a piece of aluminum foil, practice making the designs and shapes shown on the tiles. When ready, work on the tiles, starting with the C shapes and then adding leaves and dots. Make flower petals and centers last.

3. To speed the drying and cause crackling, place the tiles on foil in the oven for about 20 minutes, or until almost dry. Cool on a wire rack.

4. Apply aqua-green paint randomly to the surface and let dry. With a foam brush, apply crackle medium over the aqua areas. Let dry. Paint the tiles all over with white paint, letting the crackled areas show through. Dilute some white paint with water, and using a small round paintbrush, fill in any cracks and crevices. Dilute the cream paint with water, and lightly wash over the tiles with the brush. Let dry overnight.

5. Spray the cherubim tiles with matte sealer.

TIP Let the tiles dry thoroughly between steps. If you wish, attach a metal hanger to the back of the wood tiles at the beginning of the project. The finished pieces are very fragile and you will want to avoid hammering on them.

The original "spice girl," Kitchen Spice likes to be where the action is—and in many homes that's the kitchen. Hang her on the wall or perch her on a shelf, and she'll flutter her bay leaf wings at you flirtatiously while meals are made, snacks are shared, and coffee is "klatsched." A delicious blend of pungent spices, she's got what it takes to add some zest to your life.

Artist: Livia McRee

Kitchen Spice

1. For the body, gather all but one of the cinnamon sticks into a bunch, and tie with cord or twine. Glue the sticks tightly together at the top and splay them slightly at the bottom.

2. Peel some bark off the reserved cinnamon stick until only one layer remains. Cut and shape this core piece with scissors to make two arms. Glue the arms onto the sides of the body.

3. Glue the nutmeg to the top of the cinnamon stick body for a head. Pick off three pods from the star anise, and glue the remaining cluster of five pods to the head for a halo. Smear some glue on the nutmeg and sprinkle with coriander seeds for hair; spread the seeds out before the glue dries.

4. For a necklace, glue small mung beans over the seam between the cinnamon sticks and the nutmeg. Glue the bay leaves to her back, overlapping the ends, to make wings (see photo inset). Glue two cardamom pods to the bottom of the cinnamon stick body for feet.

5. Make a hanging loop out of cord or twine and glue it to the back of the angel above the wings.

MATERIALS
FOR 4½" (11 CM) ANGEL

- 5 or 6 cinnamon sticks
- 1 whole nutmeg
- 1 star anise
- 2 bay leaves
- 2 cardamom pods
- whole coriander seeds
- mung beans
- cord or twine
- tacky glue or hot-glue gun
- general craft supplies

TIP Use tweezers to more easily place the beans for the necklace or to precisely adjust the coriander seeds along the hairline.

View from back

Artist: Betty Auth

Guardian Angel

Everyone can use a guardian angel to protect them and offer words of inspiration.

Mixing and matching prints, playing with texture and color, and creating different ethnic looks are all part of the fun when making this angel. Put her together for a friend in need or hang her up at home. Either way, her beautiful brown eyes are sure to notice any trouble haunting the horizon.

MATERIALS

FOR 10" × 19" (25 CM × 48 CM) ANGEL

- fabric scraps in three coordinating prints plus a skin tone of your choice
- 18" × 22" (46 cm × 56 cm) unbleached muslin (a "fat quarter")
- lace trim or other embellishment
- narrow metallic ribbon
- 6" × 9" (15 cm × 23 cm) off-white felt
- small plastic curtain ring
- iron-on quilting fleece
- acrylic paints for eyes and mouth
- colored chalk or blush
- hand-appliqué needle
- sewing machine
- general craft/sewing supplies
- templates A–E (page 114)

1. Tape template A to a protected work surface. Tape the skin-tone fabric on top. Using a fine-tip permanent marker, lightly trace the facial features. Paint the eyes and lips as desired. Paint the whites of the eyes, and add highlights to the eyes and mouth. Apply pink chalk or blush to the cheeks and above the eyes, and blend with your fingertip. Add gray or brown shadows just above the eyes and around the base of the nose and the smile lines, and blend in. Use the marker to scribble in the eyelashes, rather than drawing them individually. Curve the lashes slightly.

2. Arrange templates A–E on the paper side of iron-on fleece. Trace A, B, C, and D once and E twice (flip the template over the second time). Cut out each shape. Fuse fleece cutout A to the back of the face prepared in step 1. Fuse D to the same skin-tone fabric. Fuse B, C, and both E's to the wrong sides of the three different fabrics. Cut out each piece 1" (3 cm) beyond the edge of the fleece all around.

3. Pin each piece from step 2, fabric side down, to muslin. Stitch alongside the fleece edge all around. Trim off the excess ¼" (5 mm) beyond the stitching line. Use a seam ripper to cut a small slit in the muslin of each piece, enlarge the opening to 2" (5 cm), and turn right side out. Stitch a line between the hands as shown, and darken with chalk. Hand-stitch metallic ribbon to the halo in radiating lines.

4. To assemble the angel, appliqué the hands to the heart. Tack the halo, heart, and wings to the back of the head, spacing the wings 2" (5 cm) apart. Cut a heart-shaped felt backing and sew in place to conceal the stitching and overlaps (see photo inset). Tack a curtain ring to the back for a hanger. Finish with lace embellishment around the face.

> **TIP** Because the parts are made individually before being stitched together, you can make the face on a separate piece of fabric and experiment until you're happy with it. The featured angel has an African appearance, but she can be drawn as any ethnicity.

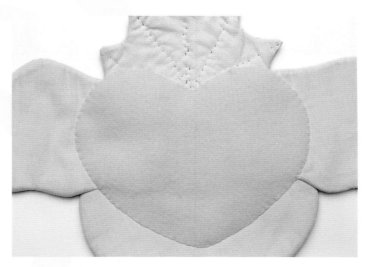

View from back

Artist: Sue Eyet

Dieter's Delight

If you've ever been on a diet, you are all too familiar with eating steamed vegetables noon and night. So take apart that tired old vegetable steamer and put it to better use: A pair of its "petals" makes an ideal set of angel wings. The Dieter's Delight angel is glad to inspire the dieter in you, but will also discreetly look the other way while you eat a cookie or two.

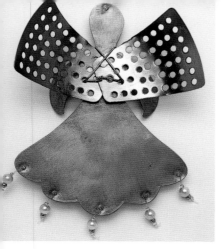

View from back

MATERIALS
FOR 5" (13 CM) ANGEL

- copper roof flashing
- old or new metal vegetable steamer
- monofilament fishing line (15 lb. test)
- ³/₈" (9 mm) No. 3 copper tacks
- 18- or 20-gauge copper wire
- assorted beads
- matte polyurethane
- rubber cement
- liquid hand or dish soap and scouring pad
- small hammer
- needle-nose pliers
- floral shears
- scratch awl or ice pick
- small anvil or steel plate
- pattern (below)

1. Disassemble a metal vegetable steamer using needle-nose pliers. Using floral shears, trim and round off the slotted area of two steamer petals.

2. Trace the angel pattern (below left) on tracing paper. Affix the tracing to the copper flashing with rubber cement. Using floral shears, cut away the bulk of the waste copper first. Then make a final detailed cutout of the angel body, taking care to prevent burrs. Peel away the tracing paper, rub off the cement, and hammer the copper cutout flat on a small anvil. Clean all three metal pieces with a scouring pad and liquid soap, working in a circular motion.

3. Punch seven holes in the angel (see pattern) using a hammer and awl. Flip the angel wrong side up and tap each hole with the hammer to flatten the rough edges.

4. To rivet the wings to the body, insert a copper tack through the angel's chest hole, front to back. On the reverse side, slip the tack through the top hole at the narrower end of each wing. Place the entire assembly facedown on a small anvil. Gently tap the copper tack with the hammer to flatten it out.

5. Gently bend the angel's arms forward, shaping them into a rounded position. If you wish, small-gauge wire may be added across the chest and secured by twisting together at the back of the angel (see photo inset). Dangle beads from the scalloped hem by threading them onto fishing line. Create a hanger from fishing line and beads, and tie it to the hole at the top of the head.

6. Give the angel a final rubbing with a scouring pad to remove any fingerprints and shine the surface. Seal with a coat of matte polyurethane. If you prefer an aged finish, omit the sealer coat and let the copper tarnish naturally over time.

> **TIP** Since most tools are sized for men's hands, they can be difficult for women to use. Floral shears make a great substitute tool for cutting lightweight metal. They fit a woman's hands well and also cut a smoother edge than most metal shears.

Angel

Artist: Sue Eyet

The Sugar Shell Angel gets her unique name from the shell-shaped sugar spoon that serves as her halo. A testament to how art can reside in the simplest of objects, this angel enjoys the domestic side of life. Hung in a bedroom or out on the patio, she'll add a sense of comfort and warmth to everything—and everyone—close by.

Sugar Shell Angel

MATERIALS
FOR 6½" (17 CM) ANGEL

- 1-lb. (.45-kg) tomato sauce can (this artist used Hunt's)
- copper roof flashing
- 36-gauge brass tooling foil
- silver-plated sugar shell spoon
- seed beads
- star bead
- monofilament fishing line (10 lb. test)
- 20-gauge sterling silver wire
- rubber cement
- small handheld drill with #62 and #65 bits (this artist used a Dremel tool)
- floral shears
- small diagonal wire cutters
- small hammer
- small anvil or steel plate
- riveting jig (see box at right)
- double-coated tape (narrow tape on dispenser works best)
- scouring pad
- can opener
- small needle-nose pliers
- patterns A, B, and C (page 19)

1. Trace patterns A, B, and C on tracing paper. Affix A to the copper flashing with rubber cement. Using floral shears, cut away the bulk of the waste copper first. Then make a final, detailed cutout along the angel outline, taking care to prevent burrs. Peel away the tracing paper, rub off the rubber cement, and hammer the copper cutout flat on a small anvil. To finish the metal surface, rub with a scouring pad.

2. To prepare the recycled tin, remove the top and bottom from a tomato sauce can, using a can opener that removes the entire end, including the rim. Carefully cut along the seam with floral shears and hammer flat. Affix tracing B to the flattened tin with rubber cement. Affix tracing C to the brass tooling foil. Using a dull pencil, mark a curlicue pattern on the C wings. Cut out B and C as in step 1.

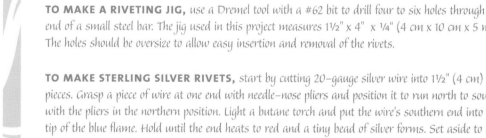

TO MAKE A RIVETING JIG, use a Dremel tool with a #62 bit to drill four to six holes through one end of a small steel bar. The jig used in this project measures 1½" x 4" x ¼" (4 cm x 10 cm x 5 mm). The holes should be oversize to allow easy insertion and removal of the rivets.

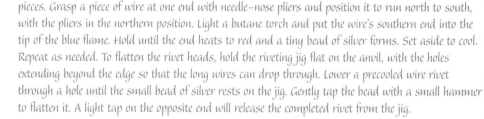

TO MAKE STERLING SILVER RIVETS, start by cutting 20-gauge silver wire into 1½" (4 cm) pieces. Grasp a piece of wire at one end with needle-nose pliers and position it to run north to south, with the pliers in the northern position. Light a butane torch and put the wire's southern end into the tip of the blue flame. Hold until the end heats to red and a tiny bead of silver forms. Set aside to cool. Repeat as needed. To flatten the rivet heads, hold the riveting jig flat on the anvil, with the holes extending beyond the edge so that the long wires can drop through. Lower a precooled wire rivet through a hole until the small bead of silver rests on the jig. Gently tap the bead with a small hammer to flatten it. A light tap on the opposite end will release the completed rivet from the jig.

TIP *Wear leather gloves to prevent cuts when working with the recycled tin—cut metal is as sharp as glass.*

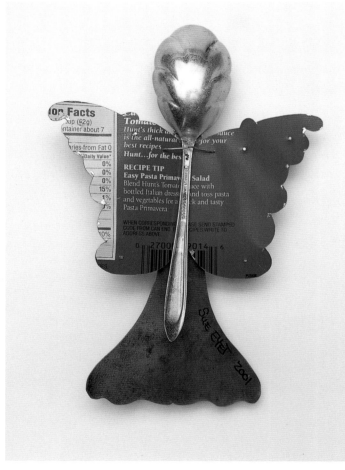

Wing and spoon attachment

3. Test-fit wing C on wing B, and join with double-coated tape. Referring to pattern C, use a #65 bit to drill a small hole at each wing tip (four holes total) through both layers. Insert a rivet through each set of holes. Turn the assembly over onto the flat surface of a small anvil. To ensure a snug fit, press down at each join and clip away the excess wire with diagonal wire cutters, leaving about $1/16$" (2 mm) of the rivet extending. Complete the riveting by gently tapping the extruding end with a hammer until flat. Drill the two remaining holes shown on the pattern if you wish to add a hanger.

4. Test-fit the body on the wings, and join with double-coated tape. Hold the taped-together angel over the spoon, centering her head over the spoon's bowl. Turn the assembly over, and locate and mark the position of the first rivet hole on the spoon handle. (It should appear at the center of the angel's chest when viewed from the front.) Remove and drill the spoon as marked, using a #65 bit. Reposition the angel over the spoon, turn the assembly over, and using the predrilled hole as a pilot hole, drill from the back through the spoon, wings, and body.

5. Insert a rivet front to back through the angel, wings, and spoon. Rivet together as in step 3. Drill a second hole 1/4" (5 mm) below the first one through all the pieces and repeat the riveting process.

6. Cut a 6" (15 cm) piece of fishing line. String on enough seed beads to wrap around the neck and extend to the chest. Bring the ends together and insert both through one seed bead, a star bead, and another seed bead. Separate the line ends and add three to four seed beads to each strand. Wrap the surplus line under each arm to the back of angel, and tie together in a knot.

7. To hang the angel, cut a piece of 20-gauge silver wire, bend it into a V shape, and insert the ends through the two extra wing holes drilled in step 3 (see photo inset). Use needle-nose pliers to grasp each end and curl it into a small loop until secure.

VARIATION *Beaded hands may be added by drilling holes as noted on the pattern prior to assembly.*

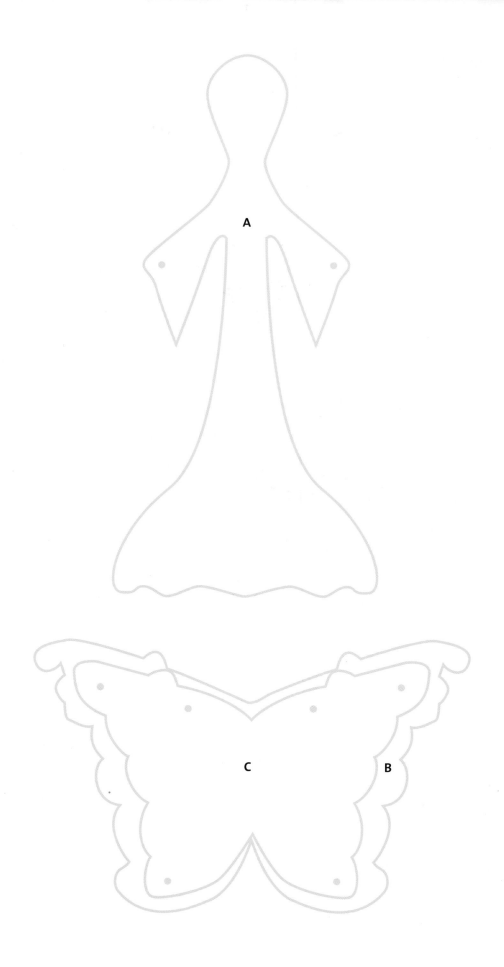

A

C   B

Artist: Suzi Carson

With her vintage linen apron and bouquet of moss and flowers, the Domestic Bliss Angel understands the joys of hearth and home. Who knew a couple of rusty wires and fabric scraps could add up to such a pretty package? She's the ideal ornament for a sunny window, watching over your kitchen as you bake the perfect pie or keeping her eye on the tulips and daylilies growing in the garden out back.

Domestic Bliss Angel

MATERIALS
FOR 5½" (14 CM) ANGEL

- 16- or 18-gauge rusty wire for body
- 20-gauge or light rusty wire for arms
- plastic-coated wire (white or a color) for wings
- fine wire (26-gauge or higher) for binding parts together
- monofilament
- 12" × 12" (30 cm × 30 cm) colorful printed vintage cotton fabric
- 12" × 12" (30 cm × 30 cm) vintage linen fabric
- small artificial flowers (roses, forget-me-nots, etc.)
- ¼" (5 mm) pearl
- green dried florist's moss
- hot-glue gun
- wire cutters
- needle-nose and regular pliers
- sewing machine, or needle and thread
- general craft supplies

1. Cut one 12" (30 cm) length each from the body, arm, and wing wires (all but the fine wire). For the body, bend the heavier rusty wire twice around a fat pencil or wooden dowel to shape a head approximately ½" (1 cm) in diameter. Twist two or three times to form a neck, and remove the dowel. Lay the two remaining wires across the body armature at the base of the neck. Bind a piece of fine wire around them in an X pattern, wrapping several times in one direction, and then several times in the opposite direction, until secure. End off by twisting together, snipping off the excess, and tucking in the ends with needle-nose pliers.

2. Cut the wires so that each arm is 2" to 3" (5 cm to 8 cm) long, each wing is 3" to 4" (8 cm to 10 cm) long, and the legs are even. Curve the rusty arm wires into a circle and bind the ends together at the front. Use needle-nose pliers to shape each white wire into a coil, suggesting a wing.

3. Tear the vintage cotton to the desired size for the skirt. Gather one edge by hand or machine to fit around the angel's waist, and glue in place, opening at the back. Bind the entire waist with 26-gauge wire. Tear an apron shape and a narrow strip from the vintage linen. Use the strip to tie the apron onto the angel, concealing the wire binding. Hot-glue flowers and green moss to the arms at front like a bouquet.

4. Thread a length of monofilament through the head. Make a knot ½" (1 cm) above the head. String on the pearl bead for a halo, and secure with a second knot.

TIP *When you can, use recycled fabrics, wire, and other found materials, which give the angels a vintage look.*

Wing placement

Sporting grapevine wings and a rustic prairie dress, the Home and Hearth Angel will add charm to any home. A tidy apron attests to her handiness at all things domestic, and an angelic face to her good nature. When you need a perfect something to bring to a housewarming party, put her at the top of your list.

Home and Hearth Angel

MATERIALS
FOR 11" (28 CM) ANGEL

- 12" × 20" (30 cm × 51 cm) muslin
- 12" × 20" (30 cm × 51 cm) calico fabric for dress
- 6" × 8" (15 cm × 20 cm) contrasting fabric for apron, dress ties, and hair ribbon
- purchased twig wings, 6" to 8" (15 cm to 20 cm) across
- fabric paint in black and white
- blush
- jute cord
- fiberfill
- hot-glue gun
- tea or coffee
- general sewing supplies
- templates A–D (page 115)

1. Fold the muslin in half, right side in, and place templates A, B, and C on top. Lightly trace around A once, B and C twice. Cut apart, but don't cut out. Machine-stitch on the marked lines through both layers, leaving the short straight edges open for turning. Cut out 1/8" (3 mm) beyond the marked line all around, and turn right side out. For an antiqued look, dip the body parts in hot tea or coffee and let dry. Stuff the body, arms, and legs with fiberfill to within 1" (3 cm) of the opening. Machine-stitch the limbs to the body, closing the openings as you go.

2. For the dress, fold the calico fabric in half, right side in. Place template D on top, and trace all around. Cut out on the marked line. Machine-stitch the side and sleeve seams through both layers, tacking at the shoulder dot. Hem the lower edge. Turn right side out.

3. For the apron, cut a 6" × 6" (15 cm × 15 cm) piece of contrasting fabric. Fold the top edge 1/2" (1 cm) to the wrong side, enclose a 10" (25 cm) strand of jute in the fold, and stitch to form a casing. Do not hem the lower edge. From the same fabric, cut three 1/2" × 6" (1 cm × 15 cm) strips for sleeve ties and a hair bow. Dye all the pieces with tea or coffee, as in step 1.

4. Use a fine paintbrush to dab two dots of black paint on the face for eyes. Let dry. Use a cotton swab to blush the cheeks. For hair, cut thirteen 10" (25 cm) jute strands, and separate the plies. Fold three plies in half and hot-glue the midpoint to the head. Continue until the head is covered.

5. Mark a shoe outline on each leg. Paint the shoes black and let dry. Dab on dots of white paint for buttons.

6. Slip the dress on the angel, and tuck in the raw edges at the neckline. Tie a fabric strip from step 3 around each wrist, and trim. Tie on the apron just under her armpits, and fluff up the casing edge. Hot-glue the twig wings to the back of the dress. Tie the remaining strip from step 3 in a bow, and hot-glue to the hair.

Artist: Kathy Cano-Murillo

When your little angels can't sleep because of bad dreams, let the Dream Protector take care of them in the wee hours. She's from a family of Amazon warrior angels whose vocation it is to protect the innocents of the world. Fun to make from a tissue roll holder, painted corn husks, and lots of glue and glitter, she'll enchant her wards with her starry robes and magical nature.

Dream Protector

MATERIALS
FOR 9 1/2" (24 CM) ANGEL

- 1 package of corn husks
- empty tissue roll
- white opalescent glitter glue
- 1 1/2" (4 cm) wooden ball
- 4" x 4" (10 cm x 10 cm) wood base
- 1 1/2" (4 cm) wooden star cutout
- 26-gauge wire
- wooden skewer
- black yarn
- 6" (15 cm) piece of lace
- clear seed beads
- silver glitter
- silver stars
- clear rhinestones
- canvas paper or light cardboard for hands
- acrylic paints in white, fuchsia, green, and light tan
- silver paint pen
- water-based varnish
- craft glue
- hot-glue gun
- handheld drill with medium bit
- general craft supplies

1. Hot-glue a layer of corn husks vertically around the tissue paper roll, pointy tips toward the top, for the angel's body. Cut two small pieces of husk for the arms, and glue them crossed over her chest in a diagonal downward position. For the robe, glue a husk on her right and left sides, letting them hang from the shoulders and drape slightly over the arms. Leave the front of the robe open.

2. For each wing, bend one husk gently in half and glue the ends together. Glue the wings to the back, checking that they appear even when viewed from the front. Add another husk over the back of the wings to complete the robe. Paint the entire body, robe, and wings white. Let dry. Apply a thin layer of white glitter glue.

3. Cut hands out of canvas paper or cardboard. Paint the hands and the wooden ball tan, and let dry. Use a liner brush to paint the face. Varnish all three pieces.

4. Drill a hole at the bottom of the head for the skewer, and glue it in place. Stand upright to dry. For hair, cut thirty 10" to 12" (25 cm to 30 cm) strands of yarn. Tie them together at the middle with another piece of yarn, and glue to the top of the angel's head. Sprinkle with glitter.

5. Slide the ball-and-skewer piece into the angel body, and glue in place. Wrap a lace scarf around the neck to hide the glue. Arrange the angel's hair to your liking, and then glue stars and rhinestones randomly to her robe and wings. Glue the hands to the arms.

6. For a halo, string seed beads onto a 5" (13 cm) piece of 26-gauge wire. Twist the ends together, shape into a circle, and place on her head. Paint the wooden star white. Coat it with glue, and sprinkle with seed beads to cover. Glue a silver star in the center. Glue and wire the star to her head.

7. Paint the wood base fuchsia, and seal with varnish. When completely dry, embellish with silver paint pen and more rhinestones. Using strong craft glue, attach the angel to the base.

TIP *Always make sure that the paint, glue, and varnish are completely dry before moving on to the next step.*

Artist: *Shirley DeLisi*

Wing placement

MATERIALS
FOR 13" (33 CM) ANGEL

- ½ yard (.5 m) cotton muslin fabric
- yarn or purchased hair curls
- purchased angel wings
- flexible dried flowers for halo
- tulle for dress
- small cloth flowers (roses or other)
- assorted ribbons
- fiberfill
- fabric paint
- sewing machine
- general sewing supplies
- templates A, B, and C (opposite page)

Sweet Pea Angel

In her gauzy white dress with its flowing pink and purple ribbons, the Sweet Pea Angel looks as though she'd be right at home entertaining wood nymphs and fairies in a little garden cottage. She delights in the outdoors, so in the house you'll want to keep her near a vase brimming with flowers or by a potted ficus. She'll thank you by making sure your flowers bloom and your plants stay lush and green.

1. Fold the muslin in half, right side in, and place the templates on top. Trace around A once and B and C twice. Cut out on the marked lines. Without separating the pieces, machine-stitch each pair ⅛" (3 mm) from the edge all around, leaving the straight edge open for turning. Turn the pieces right side out, stuff firmly, and sew closed. Join the arms and legs to the body.

2. To embellish the head, sew on the yarn or hair curls, and style as desired. Paint a face with fabric paints.

3. For the dress, assemble several layers of tulle one-and-a-half to two times the angel's waist measurement. Gather one edge by hand or machine and tack it to her waist. Wrap tulle around her torso and arms, tacking as needed. Add ribbon "cuffs" at the wrists. Crisscross the bodice with colorful ribbons, front and back, letting the streamers dangle down. Cinch the waist with another ribbon, tying it in a bow at the back. Add roses or other embellishments as desired.

4. For the halo, twist the dried flowers into a band (or wrap the stems around a pipe cleaner), and sew in place on the angel's head.

5. Sew the wings to the angel's back, hiding the stitches with more bows (see photo inset).

TIP An angel can provide a healing experience for the person creating it as well as for the person who receives it as a gift. In choosing your fabrics and embellishments, draw upon the healing powers of color and elements from nature to give your doll strength.

B
Arm
Make 2

A
Body
Make 1

C
Leg
Make 2

A colorful take on traditional corn husk dolls, with her pink dress and skeletal-leaf wings, this angel is more than a simple rose-cheeked beauty. Write a word that's important to you on a small piece of paper, fasten it to her breast before making the dress, and let "love," "hope," or "devotion" become her heart and soul.

Rose Angel

MATERIALS
FOR 9½" (24 CM) ANGEL

- natural and dyed corn husks*
- 3 packages of dark blonde doll hair
- eight 6" (15 cm) bleached and skeletonized leaves for wings
- bits of fern
- carpet and buttonhole thread
- 24-gauge stem wire
- white floral tape
- soft cloth strips
- glue

* purchased or dyed at home with RIT; see the Product Resource Guide

1. Soak the corn husks for 10 to 15 minutes in lukewarm water. Blot with paper towels.

2. For the head, put three cotton balls in the center of a piece of husk. Fold the longer edges over the cotton balls. Pinch and twist one end of the husk, fold it down to meet the opposite end, and tie together with carpet or buttonhole thread under the enclosed cotton balls.

3. For the arms, cut an 11" (28 cm) piece of stem wire, turn in the ends ½" (1 cm), and wrap with white floral tape. Read the tip on page 31 about how to tie on the husks. To make the first arm, place one end of the wire on a 6" (15 cm) piece of husk, letting the husk overhang it. Roll the husk around the wire, and tie the inner end securely. Fold the extending husk back on itself and tie at the "wrist" to form a hand. Make an arm and hand at the other end of the wire in the same way.

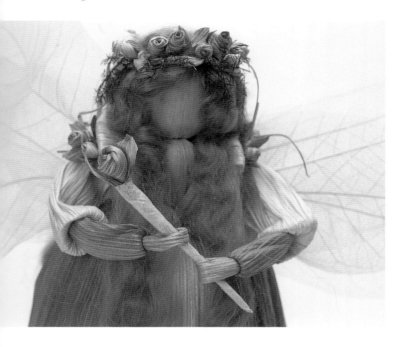

4. For the sleeves, wrap a pink husk around each lower arm, overlapping the long edges. Pinch and tie snugly at the wrist. Invert the husk and draw it back up over the arm, concealing the tying thread. Tie at the upper end to secure. Tie on a natural husk 1½" (4 cm) above each hand in the same way to make the contrasting upper sleeves.

5. For the loop trim, fold two natural husks lengthwise into strips ½" (1 cm) wide. Bring the edges together to create two 2"-long (5 cm) loops. Tie one loop to the top of each arm, and trim off the excess.

6. Center the arm piece under the head, in between the husk ends. Tie the husk ends together, locking the arm piece in place. Tie your message over the heart area with a crisscross of thread.

7. For the bodice, hold the narrow end of one husk against the breast, letting the broader end extend over the head. Tie 1½" (5 cm) below the neck. Tie on a husk at the back in the same way. Tie around both pieces at the neck, and then fold them down and tie at the waist. Make two more folded strips (as in step 4), crisscross them at the bodice, and tie at the waist. Bend the arms up out of the way, and tie with a soft cloth.

8. For the skirt, fold in the long edges of two pink husks ½" (1 cm). Hold one piece against each side of the body, and tie at the waist. Be sure to position the husks so the fullest part will fall at the bottom of the skirt and the folds will be on the inside when the husks are turned down. Place ten to twelve natural husks at 1" (3 cm) intervals around the doll's waist, and tie on. Repeat this process with two or three more layers of ten to twelve husks. Turn down the husks one by one to shape and form the skirt. Tie down with a cloth strip and let dry. To complete the skirt, untie the arms and bend them back into position. Trim the bottom of the skirt straight across with scissors, so the angel stands without rocking.

9. For each wing, assemble a small "bouquet" of four skeletonized leaves. Place the two wings together and tie at the middle. Glue the tied middle section to the angel's back.

10. Glue doll hair to the angel's head. For a halo, cover a piece of stem wire with white floral tape, shape it into a circle to fit her head, and glue in place. Add bits of fern, green corn husk leaves, tiny roses (made by twisting narrow strips of pink husk), and ribbons of husk (made by running scissors up the husk ribs). Glue more roses under the loops on the arms.

11. For her torch, bend a 5" (13 cm) length of wire back on itself and wrap with white floral tape. Cut a piece of husk 1" (3 cm) wide, fold in half lengthwise, and curl it around the torch, adding leaves and roses as you go. Bind with more tape to hold in place.

> **TIP** Corn husk has a smooth, shiny side and a dull, ribbed side. This angel is made with the smooth side showing. Making a corn husk doll is easier if you keep in mind that the husk is almost always placed in the opposite direction of its final position, tied with thread, and then turned back.

View from back

Although she's not even as tall as a tulip, the Art Deco Garden Angel adds a touch of drama wherever she is, with her streamlined copper wings and bold geometry. An expert in the art of plant care, she'll inspire gardeners at every level. And the good news for those who aren't accomplished in the garden? There's no watering required to keep her looking her best.

Art Deco Garden Angel

MATERIALS
FOR 8" (20 CM) ANGEL

- 36-gauge embossable copper sheet
- 12" (30 cm) 14-gauge copper wire
- two-part epoxy or heavy-duty indoor/outdoor clear household cement
- liquid metal cleaner
- scouring pads
- embossing stylus with small and large round ball heads
- bone folder or wooden tongue depressor
- needle-nose pliers
- wire cutters
- old scissors, including manicure scissors
- protective gloves
- general craft supplies
- patterns A and B (page 115)

1. Sandwich the copper sheet between two sheets of white paper on a smooth, flat work surface. Rub the surface with a bone folder until the copper is flattened.

2. Tape patterns A and B to the copper. Slip a thick pad of newspaper underneath. Lightly trace the outline of each shape and the designs in the interior with the small embossing stylus. Cut out both metal shapes with old scissors, using manicure scissors for the head and neck. Repeat step 1 on newspaper padding to smooth the edges and flatten the shapes.

3. Use the large embossing stylus to trace over the interior designs. Make several passes to get a good impression, letting the stylus run off the edge of the metal. To flatten the copper wings after embossing, turn the piece over and, wearing gloves, run your finger from the tip of each wing in toward the middle.

4. Shine the copper wire and cutouts with metal cleaner. Do a dry run of the step 5 assembly, note the sections that will be joined, and roughen them up with fine sandpaper or a heavy-duty scouring pad. Wipe off any lingering particles with rubbing alcohol.

5. Lay the wings face up on the newspaper. Run a bead of cement along the embossed center line. Set one end of the wire into the cement, perpendicular to the wings, to form a T shape. Tape down the other end, and let cure at least 4 hours.

6. Lay the body facedown on the newspaper. Run a bead of cement down the center. Apply more cement to the wings at the wire join. Position the wings facedown on the body so that the wire is between the two pieces and runs down the back of the angel figure. Let cure at least 12 hours.

7. Fold the arms forward on the embossed fold line and curve them into position. Poke the copper wire directly into a potted plant or vase, or coil the end and cement it to a rock or other heavy base.

VARIATIONS *Copy the patterns at different sizes to make smaller versions that can be used as ornaments or in a shadow box. To make a hanging angel, omit the wire stake and simply glue the wings directly to the body with a generous dollop of cement. Attach a loop of 24–gauge wire to the wings through holes punched with a T–pin or small brad nail. Please note: These figures are fragile and have sharp edges—they are not child-friendly.*

How do you make a physical representation of a metaphysical being? What, exactly, does an angel look like? Let's face it, there aren't any patterns available for making angels with faces of lightning and wings of thunder, and there aren't any photographs of real-life seraphim. All we have to go on is imagination.

It is imagination that wants to name the force behind the wind, the pull of the tides, the reason the sun sets only to rise again. Since the sixteenth and seventeenth centuries, people have relied on scientific explanations for these phenomena. But even a scientific mind can be charmed by the idea that it's an angel flitting through the forest that keeps it lush and green or a quartet of angels that determine the seasons.

In League with Nature

The angels in this second chapter are all linked in some way to the natural world. There are seasonal angels whose gowns are made of summer sand or autumnal moss and leaves; an angel made of bark and twigs and another with unusual bamboo wings that demonstrate the versatility of these materials; and there's an angel whose crystal head and wooden wings evoke a vision of woodlands covered in early morning dew. Separately, these angels offer glimpses into the friendlier side of nature; together, they revel in the beauty and inspiration that are found there.

Maia, Springtime Angel

Channel your spring fever into a little angel making, and tackle the Springtime

Angel, made with basic printmaking techniques. Create textures out of spring

flowers, cork, and pressed leaves, or make stencils of your own, inspired by nature.

The result? A luminous, pigmented angel to perch on your windowsill, whose

grace conjures images of renewal and growth.

TIPS *Put a layer of felt under the damp paper when printing to ensure a clear print. Use the paint in thin layers, as too much produces a muddy print.*

MATERIALS
FOR 8½" × 13" (22 CM × 33 CM) ANGEL

- 1 sheet printmaking paper (this artist used BFK Rives)
- water-mixable oil paints
- water-mixable linseed oil
- white poster board
- PVA glue
- glue stick
- textures (cork, flowers, pressed leaves)
- handcut stencils
- blotting paper
- 2 brayers
- palette knives
- Plexiglas or glass palette, at least 9" × 12" (23 cm × 30 cm)
- basin of water
- wax paper
- rolling pin
- general craft supplies
- patterns A–J (see page 116)

1. Use a straightedge to tear the printmaking paper into pieces about 9" × 12" (23 cm × 30 cm). Soak them in cool water for 15 minutes. Take a piece out, sandwich it between sheets of blotting paper, and roll across the top with a rolling pin to extract the excess water. Place the damp printmaking paper on a flat waterproof surface.

2. Squeeze a small amount of each paint color onto the palette, and use a palette knife to mix in a drop or two of linseed oil. Roll a brayer across one of the colors to load it, and then roll the paint onto a texture or stencil. Put the inked item paint side down on the damp paper, cover with wax paper, and roll a clean brayer over the top to transfer the image. Repeat this printing process with assorted colors and textures until all of the papers are decorated to your satisfaction. Let dry.

3. Place patterns A–J on the various printed papers, slip transfer paper in between, and firmly trace the solid outline with a stylus or pencil. Be sure to mark two mirror image pieces of wings B, C, and D. Choose contrasting papers for adjacent parts, especially the wings. Cut out all the pieces with a craft knife.

4. Assemble the pieces using a glue stick. For each wing, glue C to B, and then glue D to C. For the head and neck, glue pieces E–H together, overlapping the edges as indicated on the patterns. Glue the neck to the back of the body, and then add piece I. Glue the hands to the body. Glue each wing tab behind the shoulders.

5. Place the assembled angel on poster board, lightly trace the outline, and cut out ¼" (5 mm) inside the marked lines. Use PVA glue to affix this piece to the back of the angel for extra support. Glue a long wedge-shaped piece to the back for an easel-type stand.

VARIATIONS *Gouache paints mixed with monotype base or water-based printing inks (such as Speedball) could be substituted for the water-mixable oil paints. Try printing on dry paper for a different effect.*

Artist: Heidi Harrison

Angels of the Hills

These angels are wearing the traditional dress of one of Thailand's Hill Tribes, the

Karen, and offer an international take on angel lore. Masters at surviving in the

jungle, these two will gladly keep you in their sights as you do your own adven-

turing at home and abroad. All it takes is some embroidery floss, a good desk

lamp, and a little patient sewing.

A
Pants

inseam

inseam

lower edge

B
Wing

MATERIALS
FOR TWO 8" (20 CM) ANGELS

- two 1" (3 cm) wooden doll heads
- two ¼" (5 mm) wooden dowels
- two round wood bases, 4" (10 cm) in diameter
- two 5" × 12" (13 cm × 30 cm) pieces of woven fabric in black and white
- embroidery floss in black (4 skeins), white, red, blue, yellow, dark green, and light green
- narrow bias tape in beige and black
- acrylic paints in red, pink, and a skin tone of your choice
- acrylic clear satin varnish
- craft glue
- thin craft foam
- light spackling compound or water putty
- armature wire, or any sturdy bendable wire
- bamboo or wood shavings
- T-pins
- wire cutters
- needle-nose pliers
- utility cutter or coping saw
- handheld drill
- sewing machine
- general craft/sewing supplies
- templates A and B (this page)

1. Follow the instructions for Black Forest Angel, steps 1 and 2 (page 53). For the bent leg on the male angel, loop a 7½" (19 cm) piece of wire around the dowel 2½" (6 cm) from the bottom. Bend it out and down for the knee, and form a loop at the end for his foot. Use beige bias tape to bind the armature. Mold the spackling compound to create their arms and hands and his legs. Mold a foot at the base of his dowel leg.

2. For her hair, lay a skein of black embroidery floss across a 1" (3 cm) strip of narrow black bias tape. Spread the fibers over the full length of the strip and glue down. Repeat to make a second piece. Let dry. Machine-stitch each strip with black thread to make the hair part. Glue one strip on top of her head so that the part runs from ear to ear (her face and back of head will be covered). Clip the front to make bangs. Glue the second hairpiece over the first with the part going down the middle. Trim as desired. Make his hair the same way, but trim it shorter.

3. For her dress, cut two 1½" x 10" (4 cm x 25 cm) strips of white fabric. Pull out some threads to fringe the short ends. Fold the long edges ¼" (5 mm) to the wrong size and zigzag in place. Whipstitch two long edges together a little less than halfway to make the front seam. Fold the dress in half and sew the side seams, leaving ½" (1 cm) openings near the top for armholes. Embroider the dress with colored floss. Glue red floss braids around the armholes. Dress the angel, whip the back closed, and edge the neck with red braid. Glue the angel to the wood block, cutting the dowel as needed so the dress barely skims the base.

4. For his shirt, cut two 1½" x 6" (4 cm x 15 cm) strips of black fabric. Assemble as for her dress. For his pants, cut two A pieces from the fabric. Hem the lower edges. Place the pieces right sides together and sew both crotch seams. Realign and sew the full inseam. Turn right side out. Dress the angel, gathering the pants around his waist.

5. Mark two B wings for each angel on white craft foam, and cut out. Glue thin strips of bamboo to both sides. Glue green floss braids to the curved edges. Attach the wings with glue and T-pins.

Artist: Patti Medaris Culea

Ayanna, Angel of Eternal Spring

Ayanna's Cherokee name means "everlasting bloom," and she's an angel who celebrates the floral abundance of spring. Embellished with white lace and doilies that can be dyed to match your imagination's own whimsical palette, she's versatile and satisfying to make. The "starch" in her petticoats is Mod Podge, that ubiquitous craft invention of the 1960s—and frankly, decoupage art never had it so good.

MATERIALS

FOR 11" (28 CM) ANGEL

- 18" × 22" (46" × 56") cotton fabric for head and body
- ½ yard (.5 m) 6"-wide (15 cm) lace trim
- 1 yard (.9 m) 4"-wide (10 cm) lace trim
- 1 yard (.9 m) 2"-wide (5 cm) lace trim
- 3" (8 cm) flower doily for hair
- two 3" × 5" (8 cm × 13 cm) oval doilies for wings
- lace appliqué motif from bridal shop for bodice
- fiberfill
- cardboard
- decoupage medium (this artist used Mod Podge)
- colored pencils
- fabric paints in assorted colors (this artist used Dye-Na-Flow from Rupert Gibbon & Spider)
- brown, red, and black fabric pens
- white and eye-color gel rollers
- light box
- general sewing supplies, including pinking shears
- face pattern, templates A–F (see page 43)

1. Fold the cotton fabric in half, right side in, and arrange templates A–F on top, observing the grain line on A and B. Using a pencil, trace A, B, and C once and D and E twice, allowing at least ½" (1 cm) between pieces. Cut the pieces apart, but do not cut out.

2. Stitch on the solid curved line of piece A through both layers of fabric, leaving an opening between the dots as indicated. Cut out A $^{3}/_{16}$" (4 mm) beyond the marked line all around. Use a light box to trace the facial features on the wrong side (the marked side) of piece B. (You can discard the second layer of fabric.) Cut out B $^{3}/_{16}$" (4 mm) beyond the marked outline all around. Open up piece A and pin it to B, right sides together, matching the edges. Machine-stitch on the marked lines all around. Turn the head right side out through the opening, and stuff with fiberfill. Outline the facial features, dimly visible from the wrong side, with brown fabric pen. Set aside.

3. Stitch pieces C, D, and E on the solid lines through both layers of fabric, tacking at the dots. For the body, stitch down each side, from the neck to the leg opening, and stitch across the crotch. For the arms, stitch all around, leaving a small opening as indicated. For the legs, stitch down each side, leaving the top and bottom open. Close the bottom by lining up the seams and stitching across in a curving line to suggest toes.

4. Cut out the body and legs with pinking shears to avoid clipping curves. Cut out the arms with straight-edged scissors, clipping in at the thumb. Turn all five pieces right side out. Stuff firmly. Join the legs to the body using a ladder stitch. Push the neck up into the head opening and ladder-stitch together. Attach the arms to the body, running the thread through the body from one arm to the other for a strong hold.

View from back

VARIATIONS *Ayanna can stand on her own but also looks beautiful hanging up. Mostly she likes to be around flowers. Stand her next to a vase full of your favorites.*

5. Shade the angel's face with a peach-colored pencil, and blush her cheeks with a rose-colored pencil. Color the irises, and outline them with a gel roller or fabric pen. Blacken the pupil with a pen. Color in her lips with colored pencils, then outline them with a red fabric pen. With a white gel roller, whiten the whites of the eyes, add a highlight to each pupil, and lighten the lower lip. Add eyelashes and eyebrows with a brown fabric pen. Use an iron on the cotton setting to heat-set the colors. Apply decoupage medium all over.

6. Test-fit the 4"-wide (10 cm) lace around the torso and cut off the required length. Color the laces and doilies with fabric paints. To re-create Ayanna's dress, apply yellow paint to the 2"-wide (5 cm) lace and the 4"-wide (10 cm) torso lace; violet paint to the remaining 4"-wide (10 cm) lace; and bright green paint to the 6"-wide (15 cm) lace. Let dry. Iron to set the colors.

7. For the skirt, cut one 16" (41 cm) strip of green lace, one 16" (41 cm) strip of violet lace, and one 12" (30 cm) strip of yellow lace. Gather each skirt lace along one edge with needle and thread, and then dip them in the decoupage medium. Attach the green lace at the waist, followed by the violet and yellow tiers. Saturate the yellow bodice lace with decoupage medium, and pin it in place on the body.

8. For each sleeve, cut one 6" (15 cm) piece of violet lace and one 6" (15 cm) piece of yellow lace. Gather one edge and saturate, as for the dress tiers. Attach the violet lace first and then the yellow lace around the upper arm. Cut out flowers from a lace appliqué, and apply them to the bodice with decoupage medium.

9. Paint the small flower doily yellow and scarlet. Saturate it, pin it to her head, and arrange a nice hairstyle. Saturate the two white wing doilies, attach them to her back, and hold with pins until dry. Put plastic wrap or wax paper underneath the skirt to preserve the fullness. Once the tiers of lace are dry, you'll still be able to arrange them a bit.

10. For the shoes, cut a bit of yellow lace to fit around each foot. Saturate each piece and drape it around a foot, folding at the toes. Let the shoes dry partially. Cut two soles from cardboard using template F, and color with paint or markers to match the shoes. Let dry. Apply decoupage medium to the soles and glue them to the bottom of the feet, holding with pins or clips until dry.

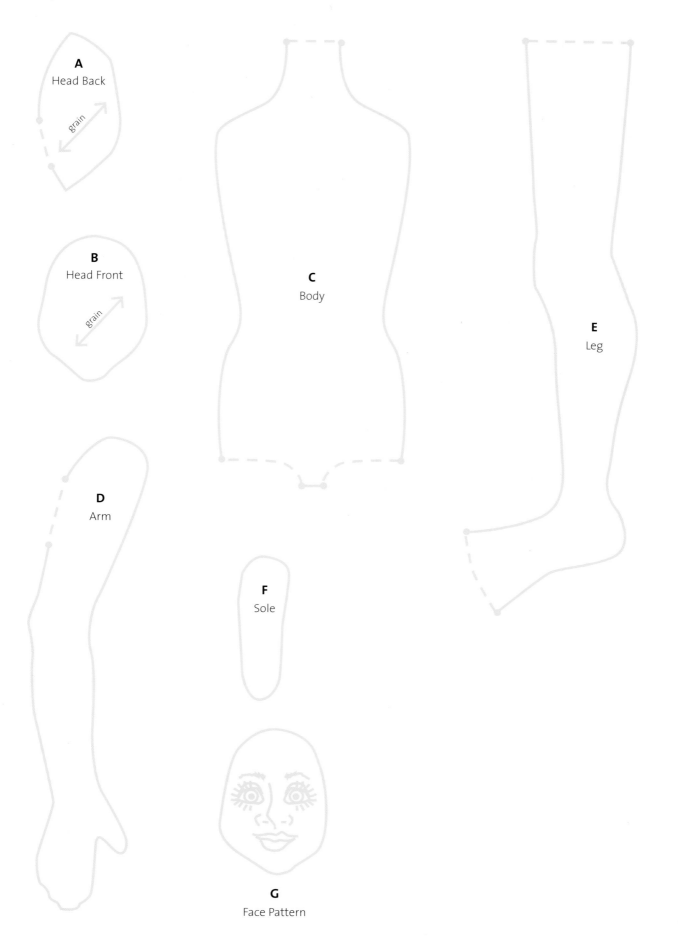

A
Head Back

grain

B
Head Front

grain

C
Body

D
Arm

E
Leg

F
Sole

G
Face Pattern

Artist: Sue Eyet

MATERIALS
FOR 7" (18 CM) ANGEL

* 8" × 10" × ½" (20 cm × 25 cm × 1 cm) pine
* silver tin (such as the inside of a popcorn can)
* 36-gauge brass tooling foil
* crystal lamp prism for head
* clear seed beads
* 4-mm glass rocaille E beads
* crystal beads
* ½" (1 cm) brass nails
* metallic gold acrylic paint
* iridescent white powdered pigment (this artist used Jacquard Pearl-Ex pigment 651 in pearl white)
* monofilament fishing line (15 lb. test)
* sawtooth hanger
* double-coated tape (narrow tape on a dispenser works best)
* hammer
* small handheld drill with #65 bit (this artist used a Dremel tool)
* embossing stylus
* floral shears
* coping saw
* templates A, B, and C (opposite page)

Crystal, Dewdrop Angel

A friend to early risers, the Dewdrop Angel's crystal face and sparkling arms make her a fitting representative of the glittering mist that covers hill and dale at daybreak. Made from an unexpected mix of materials, she reminds us to think "outside the box" and to take pleasure in the creative alchemy that transforms everyday objects into something new.

1. Trace template A onto the silver tin. Trace template B onto 36-gauge brass tooling foil. Use a stylus to mark a curlicue design on the surface of B. Using floral shears, cut away the bulk of the waste metal around both pieces. Follow up with a closer, more detailed cutting, working carefully to avoid burrs. Using double-coated tape, secure dress B to dress A.

2. Trace template C onto the pine and cut out using a coping saw. Carve along the edges with a craft knife to add interest. Mix 2 parts gold acrylic paint, 1 part white powdered pigment, and 1 part water, and sponge-paint the wings. Let dry.

3. Position the teardrop crystal prism, pointed end down, on the wings. Mark the location of the crystal's hole on the wood, drill a starter hole, and attach with a small brass nail. Position the metal dress on the wings, sliding the neck under the teardrop "chin." Attach with three brass nails down the center of the dress (see photo).

4. Drill a hole through the wooden wing at the end of one sleeve. Fold a piece of monofilament line in half, slip a seed bead on one end, and slide it to the fold. Insert both ends of the line through the sleeve hole, back to front, and pull until snug. String three glass beads, one crystal bead, and another seed bead onto both lines. Drill a second hole into the wooden wing at the point where the beads end. Insert both lines through the second hole, pull snug, and tie off through a bead at the back. Repeat to make a second arm.

5. Attach a sawtooth hanger to the back of the angel for hanging.

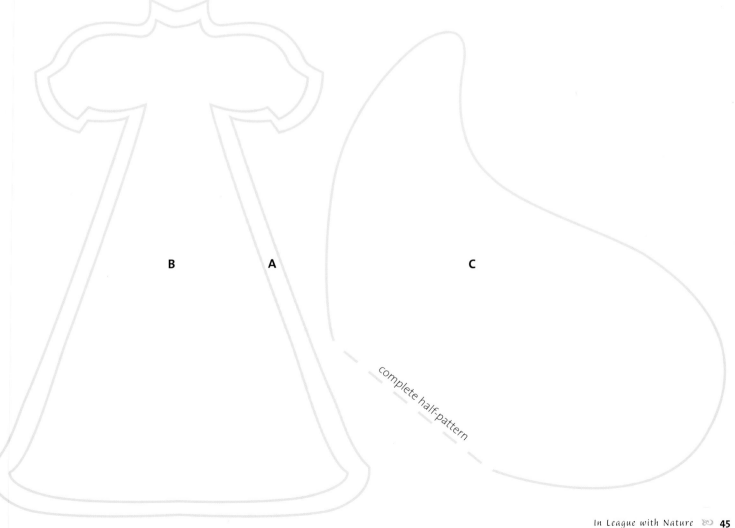

B

A

C

complete half-pattern

Artist: Paula Grasdal

What better way to conjure up the lazy days of an oceanside vacation than to turn treasures gathered at the beach into art? Made of pieces of colorful sea-smoothed glass, gritty sand, and crushed shells mounted on a clear film backing, the Summer Angel evokes the all-too-fleeting pleasures of a day of beachcombing. Put her in a window and watch the light illuminate her, bringing her vividly to life.

Summer Angel

MATERIALS
FOR 12" × 8" (30 CM × 20 CM) ANGEL

- sand in two textures or colors
- beach glass
- crushed shells
- shell fragments
- heavy Mylar polyester film
- monofilament (15 lb. test)
- two-part epoxy
- craft glue
- small embroidery scissors
- hammer and nail
- general craft supplies
- patterns A, B, and C (page 116)

1. Use a fine-point permanent marking pen to trace patterns A, B, and C, including dotted lines, onto Mylar film. Cut out, using embroidery scissors for the detailed areas. Glue B to A with epoxy, and let set for 5 minutes. Use a hammer and nail to punch a small hole at the dot in the hands through both layers (place a small block of wood underneath as a backing).

2. Lay the paper pattern B on a flat surface. Arrange the beach glass within the skirt outline in a pleasing pattern, positioning larger pieces first and fitting smaller pieces around them. Once the arrangement is determined, glue the pieces to the Mylar skirt in the same order. Use a cotton swab to apply epoxy to both the glass and the film before pressing them together. Epoxy hardens quickly, so mix up small amounts at a time.

3. Cover your work surface with newspaper. Brush craft glue onto the wings of piece A, and sprinkle with sand. Repeat for the head and the hands, using finer or colored sand for contrast. Apply a thin bead of glue along the dotted lines of piece B to define the arms, and sprinkle with fine sand. Let dry. Sprinkle off the excess.

4. Brush craft glue onto the headdress and bodice (avoiding the sand line), and cover with crushed shells. Attach shell fragments with epoxy at the base of the headdress. Using a brush, apply craft glue between the glass pieces, and sprinkle with fine sand to suggest grout. Touch up any areas on the wings or face that need more sand.

5. Cut an 18" (46 cm) length of fishing line, knot one end, and thread it through the hand hole from the front. Secure the knot with a dab of epoxy, affix the sanded hands over it, and press gently until set. Tie a loop for hanging at the other end. Let the completed angel set for 24 hours before hanging her up.

TIP *Use a contrasting color and texture for the bodice and headdress. The featured angel's bodice is made of a crushed white sand dollar to contrast with the beige sand. To crush your shells, place them on top of piece of wood between two sheets of paper, and then hammer. Be sure to wear protective goggles.*

With a face like that of a pagan goddess, the Sun-Kissed Angel revels in the glory of the sun. She's got a flexible design that can be adapted to make a flock of companion angels, and her colorful paints and glue-on beads make her a sparkling emissary for the light she loves.

Artist: Sandra McCall

Sun-Kissed Angel

MATERIALS
FOR 4" (10 CM) ANGEL

- two 4" × 4" (10 cm × 10 cm) pieces of muslin
- 4" × 8" (10 cm × 20 cm) felt
- assorted beads and embellishments
- butterfly hair clip for wings
- pin back or yarn
- rubber stamp (this artist used "Primitive Woman")
- permanent ink pen
- Fantastix paint sticks (if unavailable, use paintbrushes)
- ink pads and refills in a variety of colors plus black, for stamping fabric
- fabric glue
- craft glue and a toothpick
- plate (for palette)
- heat gun or iron (for setting ink)
- water-filled spray bottle
- general craft supplies

1. Stamp "Primitive Woman" in black ink on one piece of muslin. Heat-set the ink using a heat gun or iron. Paint the fabric using paint sticks, ink, and water, without obliterating the black stamping. Heat-set the fabric again. (Each application has to be heat-set individually to be permanent.) Set aside.

2. For the back, spray the second piece of muslin generously with water. Dab some of the refill ink colors on the palette and dilute with water. Use the paint sticks to apply the colors to the fabric, spreading them around so that they bleed together. Scrunch the fabric into a ball, smooth it out, and dry with a heat gun or by ironing.

3. Cut out the stamped image ¼" (5 mm) beyond the outline all around. Cut two corresponding felt shapes, slightly smaller and graduated in size, for filler. Lay the back piece wrong side up on the work surface. Place the felt filler on it, with the smaller piece on the top. Lay the stamped cutout facedown, and run a bead of fabric glue around the cutout edge. Set it glue side down on the assembled layers and press until the edges adhere. Let dry. Trim the back piece even with the cutout edge. Note that the back is cut *after* the pieces are glued together. This encourages the back to remain flat and the front to puff up.

4. Add fibers, beads, and embellishments with craft glue, using a toothpick to position the small pieces. If the butterfly hair clip is coated with glitter, burn it off using a torch (do this outdoors) or the open flame from an outdoor grill. Cut the two halves apart, apply fabric glue, and affix them to the angel's back. Add a pin back to wear the angel on your jacket or a loop of yarn to hang her as an ornament or decoration.

TIP Use one paint stick per ink color. That way, you won't have to stop and clean the stick every time you change colors.

A great project for one of those languid summer afternoons when hiding indoors is the only way to beat the heat, the Lazy, Hazy Day Angel is simplicity itself. Just cut her out of wood and paint her. While she dries, follow her lead, and dive into your own juicy slice of watermelon. And you won't have to hide her away when summer draws to a close—angels can always wear white.

Artist: Lorraine Gendron

Lazy, Hazy Day Angel

1. Trace the pattern on this page. Enlarge it 200% on a photocopier, to make an angel 11" (28 cm) tall. Cut out the photocopy for a template.

2. Trace around template to mark the angel on the wood. Also mark a 3" × 6" (8 cm × 15 cm) piece for the base. Cut out both shapes with a small utility cutter or coping saw.

3. Using fine-grit sandpaper, sand the wooden figure and base until smooth. Wipe clean with a cloth or rag.

4. Drill a hole in the middle of the base slightly smaller than the wooden peg. Drill a corresponding hole in the bottom edge of the angel. Glue the peg into the hole, tapping in place with a hammer. Glue the angel to the base, tapping from the underside. Let set.

5. Paint the standing angel freehand with acrylic paints, using your creativity to make her an expression of your own style of painting. Let dry overnight. Finish with a coat of matte acrylic varnish or polyurethane.

MATERIALS
FOR 11" (28 CM) ANGEL

- 13" × 20" × 1" (33 cm × 51 cm × 3 cm) piece of scrap wood
- wooden peg
- acrylic paints in assorted colors
- matte acrylic varnish or polyurethane
- wood glue
- small utility cutter or coping saw
- handheld drill
- hammer
- general craft supplies
- template (this page)

Artist: Paula Grasdal

Her beautiful red leaf wings and serene birch face make this moss-covered angel the consummate ambassador of autumn. Forage in the woods or your neighborhood craft store for materials in which to dress her. Shown here in silhouette, she seems to be flying into a crisp moonlit night, perhaps to oversee the changing of the seasons.

Fall Harvest Angel

MATERIALS
FOR 8½" (22 CM) ANGEL

- 9" × 12" (23 cm × 30 cm) foam core
- sheet moss, pressed leaves, and fern
- birch bark or wood veneer
- florist's wire
- monofilament
- PVA glue
- acrylic matte medium
- craft stick
- general craft supplies
- patterns (opposite page)

1. Trace the patterns. Place the tracing patterns on the foam core, slip transfer paper in between, and go over with a stylus to transfer the design. Transfer the arm/hand unit and the spiral shape separately. Cut out all three shapes with a craft knife.

2. Glue the arm/hand cutout to the foam-core torso. Glue the spiral cutout to the lower edge of the tunic.

3. Repeat the step 1 technique to transfer the head and hand outlines to the birch bark. Cut out the pieces carefully, making several passes to avoid chipping the bark. Glue the bark to the foam core, pressing firmly until the glue sets.

4. Working small sections at a time, brush glue onto the arm, tunic, and headdress, and attach small pieces of moss. Lightly mold the moss with your fingers around the glued-on arm and spiral for dimensional interest. Brush glue onto the edges of the foam-core shape and sprinkle with leftover moss fibers. Use a craft stick to press the fibers into the glue as it sets.

5. Transfer the wing shape to bond paper, and cut out. Brush glue onto the back of pressed autumn leaves and apply them to the wing cutout. Layer small leaves over large ones to suggest feathers. Flip the wing over and trim the overhanging leaves with scissors. Brush glue onto the foam-core wing and apply the leaf wing to it, pressing until the glue sets.

6. To make a hanger, cut a 1" (3 cm) piece of florist's wire. Curve one end into a small loop, and make an L-shaped bend at the middle. Dab a bit of glue on the straight end and stick it sideways into the foam core, with the loop at the top. Tie a length of monofilament to the wire loop for hanging.

7. Apply moss to the back of the angel as in step 4. Trim away any excess moss. Glue a narrow length of pressed fern onto the headdress. Finally, brush acrylic matte medium onto the pressed-leaf wing to protect it and bring out the colors.

TIP *Soak the bark in hot water about 15 minutes to soften it. Let it dry pressed between layers of newsprint. Take bark only from a branch on the ground, not from a living tree.*

VARIATIONS *Try decorating the angel on both sides, and hang it where both sides will be visible. Substitute pressed flowers, seeds, dried herbs, or dried grasses for the moss.*

Artist: Heidi Harrison

Hair arrangement

A true spirit of nature, the Black Forest Angel appreciates life in all its myriad forms. Her silver-trimmed wings seem ready to whisk her away at a moment's notice, but she's perfectly content to stay and bless your home as long as there's a window nearby from which to watch birds, butterflies, and other denizens of her favorite realm.

Black Forest Angel

MATERIALS
FOR 8" (20 CM) ANGEL

- 1" (3 cm) wooden doll head
- ¼" (5 mm) wooden dowel
- 1" × 1" × 1" (3 cm × 3 cm × 3 cm) wood block for base
- armature wire, or any stiff bendable wire
- thin white craft foam
- 7" × 7" (18 cm × 18 cm) soft white cotton fabric
- 9" × 14" (23 cm × 36 cm) soft printed cotton fabric
- yarn for hair
- 1 yard (.9 m) baby eyelet trim
- narrow white bias tape
- silver metallic rickrack
- acrylic paints in red, titanium white, and a skin tone of your choice
- acrylic clear satin varnish
- light spackling compound or water putty
- craft glue
- wire cutters
- pliers
- utility cutter or coping saw
- handheld drill with ¼" (5 mm) bit
- sewing machine
- general craft/sewing supplies
- wing template (page 55)

1. Drill a ¼" (5 mm) hole in the middle of the base. Cut an 8" (20 cm) piece of wooden dowel, and glue one end to the wooden doll head. Paint the head, dowel, and block in a skin tone and let dry. Draw the eyes, nose, and eyebrows with pencil. Paint the mouth red and the cheeks pink and let dry. Varnish all the pieces.

2. For the arms, cut a 13" (33 cm) piece of wire. Bend the wire back onto itself 3" (8 cm) from each end, and twist to secure. Hold the arm wire against the dowel ½" (1 cm) below the head. Wrap both arms around the dowel twice, or until each arm measures 2¾" (7 cm); adjust so that the shoulders are aligned. Apply glue to the wire join and to the dowel below it for about 1¾" (5 cm). Bind the join with narrow bias tape, wrapping in a crisscross fashion to build up the shoulders. Continue wrapping onto the glued section of the dowel to form the body. Glue and wrap each arm, stopping just before the hand loop. Paint the exposed wire loops and let dry. Apply spackling compound or putty to the loops, and mold into hands. Let dry overnight. Paint and varnish the hands.

3. For the sleeves, cut two 2" × 4" (5 cm × 10 cm) pieces of soft white cotton fabric. Fold each piece in half, right side in, and stitch the long edges together to make a tube. Turn right side out. Press the raw wrist edge to the wrong side, and hand-sew a running stitch. Slip the sleeves onto the angel's arms, and glue at the shoulders. Glue a 2" (5 cm) strip of eyelet to hold the sleeves in place and form a neckline. Finish by gathering each wrist edge.

4. For the bodice, cut two 2" × 1" (5 cm × 3 cm) strips of printed cotton fabric. Press the long edges to the wrong side. Hand-sew across middle of each strip and gather tightly to form narrow shoulders. Glue each bodice piece to the body at the shoulder. Using black thread, work a straight-stitch closure down the bodice front. Hand-sew or glue a dart in each front piece.

5. For the skirt, cut a 12" × 5" (30 cm × 13 cm) piece of printed cotton fabric. Fold in half, right side in, and sew the short edges together. Press one edge to the wrong side, and topstitch or glue to the eyelet trim (remove the bias edge from the trim first to reduce bulk). Press and topstitch two tucks in the skirt above the hemmed edge. Hand-sew a running stitch around the raw edge, gather tightly, and glue to the angel's waist, concealing the lower edges of the bodice. Glue the dowel to the base, trimming if needed so that the dress hem barely skims the base.

6. For the apron, cut a 5½" × 2¾" (14 cm × 7 cm) piece from the white cotton fabric. Stitch two overlapping rows of eyelet trim along the shorter edge. Press the long edges ¼" (5 mm) to the wrong side and topstitch. Sew a running stitch across the raw edge, gather to 3" (8 cm), and enclose in an 8" (20 cm) length of bias tape, letting the excess tape extend evenly at each end for apron ties. Glue the apron to the doll to hide the unfinished waist edge of the skirt. Tie at the back.

7. For the hair, cut a 3½" × ½" (9 cm × 1 cm) strip of fabric, paint it to match the face skin tone, and let dry. Cut about twenty 10" (25 cm) strands of yarn. Lay the scalp strip on a flat surface. Lay the yarn strands across it, close together, with the ends extending evenly on both sides. Glue in place. Let dry. Hand-sew with matching thread to accentuate the part line. Glue the scalp to the head. Style the hair with narrow braids, using matching thread to tie off the ends. Finish with pigtails or thick braids (see photo inset on page 53).

8. Use the wing template to mark two wings on white craft foam. Cut out both pieces. Paint with white acrylic paint on both sides, let dry, and seal with clear satin varnish. Glue silver rickrack to both sides, overhanging the edge. Test-fit the wings on the angel body, and bend the rickrack outward on the section that will be glued. Glue in place, holding until the glue sets, about 5 minutes.

TIP *To give the wings extra support, push a straight pin through the rickrack at the top of the glued wing section and into the angel body.*

VARIATION *For a slightly softer look, reduce the size of the wings and cover them with fabric instead of paint.*

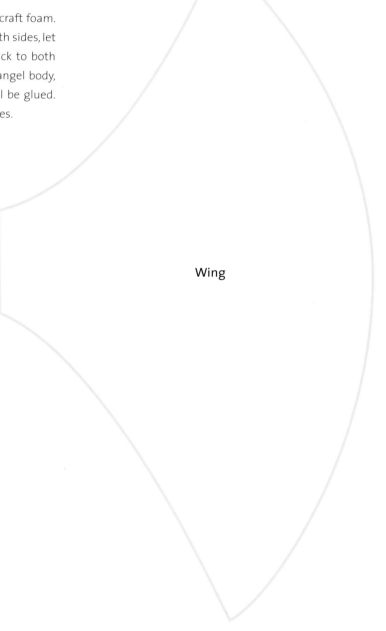

Wing

Artist: Mechtild H. Henry

Side view of hands

A study in earth tones, the Angel in Brown has a contemplative spirit and brings peace to whatever environment she graces. The flowing lines of her dried-leaf gown and a winsome mushroom halo remind us that you don't always have to yell out loud to get your point across. Just listen carefully, and she'll gladly share her secrets.

Angel in Brown

MATERIALS
FOR 10" (25 CM) ANGEL

- 4 dried *Philodendron monstera* leaves
- long strand of raffia
- dainty dried flowers
- dried mushroom for halo
- natural beads for necklace
- general craft/sewing supplies

TIP Philodendron monstera is a Central American plant that thrives in tropical and subtropical locations. The leaves used in this project are the protective sheaths the plant casts off when it grows new leaves.

1. Soak the dried leaves in tepid water until they are pliable, about 1 hour. Starting with the smaller end, fold one leaf toward you (with the crinkly side facing out), and roll it until it measures 1" (3 cm) around. This smaller end is the head. The wide, wavy end will be the back panel of the skirt.

2. Fold the second leaf, crinkly side out, around the first leaf, enclosing the head in the fold. Arrange the wavy edge of this leaf to be the bottom of the skirt's front panel (see photo). Twist the folded leaf on top of the head and guide it down the back. Tie a piece of raffia around it, wrap both ends of the raffia once around the angel's neck, and tie again at the back. Do not cut the raffia.

3. Slip the remaining two leaves, crinkly sides up, in between the front and back of the dress from each side. Pull through so that the smaller ends stick out about 3" (8 cm) at either side and the wider wavy ends look like wings.

4. Guide the raffia strands at the back neck down to the back waist, around to the front, and tie together at the front waist. Wrap each strand of raffia around the smaller ends of the wing leaves, draw them together to suggest hands, and tie again. Let the extra raffia hang down the angel's front like a monk's belt. Tie a knot in each end.

5. Assemble and insert a bouquet of flowers between the hands. Glue the hands together, holding them with a clip until the glue is dry.

6. Cut three strips of leaf fiber and braid them. Set the braid on the head, letting the ends hang loose at the back of the head. Sew it in place with a fine, long needle, and decorate it with flowers. String a necklace of natural beads and secure it around her neck.

7. Secure the mushroom "halo" to the back of the head with a few stitches and some glue. Camouflage the stitches by gluing a flower here and there. To hang the angel, attach a loop of raffia at the back.

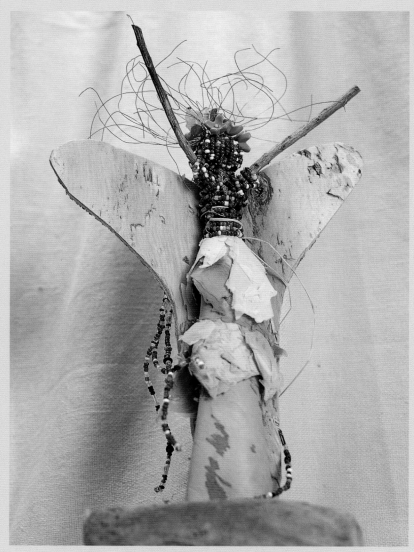

Artist: Barbara Carleton Evans

Earth Angel

Bringing the outdoors in is all the rage in design circles, and the Earth Angel makes it easy to do. Scavenge around your own backyard (or that of a friend if you're a city dweller) to find some pretty branches, and then dig around in your craft box for flowery treasures, beads, and other embellishments. Take your cue from Mother Nature in springtime and don't hold back.

TIPS *Because this design depends upon natural materials, each angel will be unique. Start with the shape of the branch and choose a base, skirt material, bodice beads, and embellishments to enhance the shape, color, and attitude of the branch. Collect twice as much bark as you think you'll need so that you have an ample selection once you are working.*

MATERIALS

FOR 10¾" (28 CM) ANGEL

- driftwood
- three-pronged branch
- thin pieces of flexible bark
- seed beads
- thin wire
- wooden bead with large center hole
- blue glass flower beads and leaves
- small handheld drill (this artist used a Dremel tool)
- pruning shears
- general craft supplies

1. To create the body, cut a three-pronged branch with pruners, trimming the middle prong for the neck and the two outside prongs for arms. Cut the main stem—the body—to a length in proportion to the arms, plus a bit extra for mounting. Drill a hole in the driftwood to accommodate the body stem. Glue it in place.

2. To add a skirt, wrap pieces of thin bark around the body and glue them in place.

3. For a bodice, string seed beads onto wire in strands about 18" (46 cm) long. Wrap the strands around the body and shoulders as desired, letting some ends dangle down. The number of strands needed will depend on the size of your branch.

4. To make the head, wrap another strand of seed beads around a wooden bead with a large center hole. Fit the head on the neck and glue it in place. Fasten blue glass flower beads and leaves to the head with fine wire for the halo. Leave the ends of the wire long and add more wire as desired to suggest fluffy hair. Curl or twist the wire as desired.

5. Cut each wing from a single piece of bark in a shape that suits the angel. Drill or pierce two tiny holes in each wing, run wire through them, and fasten the wings to the body. Add beads to the ends of the wire as decoration.

VARIATIONS *If you are unable to find appropriate tree bark for the wings, brown paper bags can be substituted.*

Artist: Paula Grasdal

If the winter doldrums have you in their grip, this ethereal angel is sure to lighten your sagging spirits. Through clever cutting and crimping of wire mesh, you can shape an inspired candlelit sculpture that will add radiance to the year's shortest day. Use the Winter Solstice Angel as a beautiful centerpiece for a cozy meal with family and friends, or place her in a window to gaze serenely at the sleeping winter world outside.

Winter Solstice Angel

MATERIALS
FOR 13" × 10" (33 CM × 25 CM) ANGEL

- copper wire mesh (this artist used "Wireform" ⅛ pattern)
- 18-gauge copper wire
- 28-gauge wire (copper or other)
- tea light candle
- small pliers and needle-nose pliers
- scissors designated for wire cutting
- hammer
- protective gloves
- general craft supplies
- patterns A–G (see page 117)

VARIATIONS *Try substituting aluminum or brass mesh for copper or combining different metals in the same project. For a whimsical touch, hang a twig inside the angel's skirt. Cover her with rice paper and watered-down glue to create a lantern.*

1. Unfold the copper mesh, lay it flat, and gently tap out the creases with a hammer. Place patterns A–G underneath the mesh, and trace the outlines with a permanent marker. Cut out the wire mesh shapes using the special scissors. Be sure to wear protective gloves.

2. Cut an 11" (28 cm) length of 18-gauge wire. Hold it along the lower curved edge of the skirt A, and bend the mesh over it for ⅛" (3 mm) with pliers. Bend back one straight edge of the skirt for a neat finish. Bend the skirt into a cone shape, overlapping the straight edges, and secure with masking tape at the middle. "Stitch" the straight edges together with 28-gauge wire, removing the tape to join the middle.

3. Mold the mesh circle B up around the tea light to make the candleholder, trimming to even up the edges. Nestle the tea light and holder in the opening at the top of the skirt. Fold the mesh edges of the holder down over the skirt to secure.

4. Bend the outside edge of piece C ⅛" (3 mm) to the wrong side. Mold the face by placing the mesh over a small rock and pulling out and shaping the features with needle-nose pliers. (A small doll's head would also work as a mold.) Hold piece D in position behind the head, and bend back the edges of the front halo to secure it. Join the skirt and torso by wrapping the torso belt around the skirt top and overlapping the ends at the back.

5. Place wing E on wing F, align the top edges, and bend back the doubled edge. Trim the lower edge of wing F to match the feather shapes of the top layer. Bend back the remaining edges ⅛" (3 mm) for a clean finish. Hold the wings in position at the back of the torso, and bend ¼" (5 mm) of the angel's shoulders over them.

6. Fold down the edge of each arm G, leaving the hands unfinished. Bend each arm over a pencil to add volume. Fold the torso back at the dotted lines, hold each arm in position, and bend the top of the arm over the wing to secure. Reinforce each shoulder join with 28-gauge wire. Place the hands together and bend the edges to join them. Align the hands with the top of the candleholder to "hold" the candle flame.

If you have ever found yourself asking, "Hey, what has an angel done for me lately?" this third chapter could prove to be enlightening.

The angels gathered here are joined together by a sense of higher purpose: They exist above the horizon of everyday life, in a place where inspiration dwells, happiness flourishes, and friendship is more than just a ten-letter word. These are the beings that inspire the singer to sing, the poet to rhyme (or not to), and the dancer to—well, you get the idea.

Above the Horizon

And what a selection of materials you'll find—lovely kimono fabric, crisply folded sheet music wings, button heads, decoupage and rhinestones, skirts and wings of iridescent ribbons and glittering trims, silver, copper, and brass wire, a popcorn tin, Mexican *milagros* and golden glitter, Mississippi mud, stained glass, coffee-dyed muslin, and paint, paint, and more paint.

More than just the sum of their varied parts, these angels are the harbingers of joy and good fortune and the champions of charity and devotion. For those souls who are looking for something more compelling than another Thursday night in front of the television, spend some time with this cast of characters. They just might help you to know your better self.

Artist: Kathy Peterson

VARIATIONS *For other unique angels, try using wallpaper, card stock, or old love letters for this project. If you can't find a cone-shaped water cup, simply cut and fold a piece of paper into a cone shape to create the template.*

The Singing Angel is the perfect gift for the music lover in your life. Replicate her in different sizes and you'll have your own celestial chorus. She perches easily on any flat surface—a mantel, a piano top, a bedroom bureau. A Gershwin tune turns her into a valentine, a gospel song into a tree ornament, a punk rock anthem into something that's just right for the rebel in you.

Singing Angels

MATERIALS
FOR EACH 4¾" (12 CM) ANGEL

- one large page of sheet music
- ½" (1 cm) two-hole black or brown button
- scrap of black felt
- gold leafing pen
- black marking pen
- hot-glue gun
- hole punch
- cone-shaped paper drinking cup
- general craft supplies

1. To make a template, cut the drinking cup along the seam and open so it lies flat. Place this template on the sheet music, trace, and cut out. Roll the sheet music cutout into a cone shape for the angel body. Overlap and glue the outside edges.

2. For the wings, cut a 4" × 5" (10 cm × 13 cm) piece of sheet music. Make accordion-style folds every ½" (1 cm) parallel to the longer edge. With the wings still folded, cut the tips at a 45° angle and punch a hole through the center. Mount the wings onto the point of the cone body, and glue in place. Let dry. Fan out the wings as desired.

3. For the arms, cut a 2½" × 5" (6 cm × 13 cm) piece of sheet music. Fold one long edge in ½" (1 cm). Fold in again two more times. Trim off the excess and glue down the outside edge. Glue the center of the arms to the back of the cone body just under the wings. Fold in each end ½" (1 cm) for hands.

4. For the hymnal, cut a small rectangle from a piece of sheet music. Outline the edges using a black marker. Fold in half, and glue to the angel's hands.

5. For the head, use the button. Picture the two button holes as eyes, and use a marking pen to draw in a mouth and hair in a contrasting color. Glue the button head to the top of the cone body just above the wings. Cut a small bow tie from felt, and glue it at the neck.

TIPS *When working with vintage sheet music, be sure you are not destroying a coveted antique piece. Paper tends to deteriorate with age, so be selective when choosing paper to make your angel. You could also use a photocopy. Use a gentle touch when tracing your pattern, so that if you make a mistake, you can easily erase it.*

A vision in her blue and silver gown, the Poetry Lover's Angel is as beautiful as the verse she celebrates. In the same way a poet stitches together simple words to find a deeper truth, she's crafted from the most prosaic of materials: cardboard, metal foil, a handful of beads, a scrap of fabric. Make her for the poetry lover in you or in your life.

Poetry Lover's Angel

MATERIALS
FOR 20" (51 CM) ANGEL

- angel in profile (see step 1)
- sea-green lightweight metal foil
- 10" × 13" (25 cm × 33 cm) coordinating fabric
- metallic thread
- miniature glass beads in silver
- 1-ply cardboard
- embellishing adhesive
- white glue or PVA glue
- hot-glue gun
- verdigris embossing powder
- embossing heat tool
- general craft/sewing supplies
- wing template (page 118)

1. Choose an angel image in profile to use for the head and torso (the featured image is Gustav Klimt's *Die Musik*, taken from a calendar). Make two photocopies—one as is, and one as a reverse image, for a two-sided angel. Cut out both profiles carefully using a sharp craft knife.

2. Mount one image on a piece of lightweight cardboard with white glue. Trim the cardboard to the outline of the figure, leaving some excess cardboard below the torso for mounting the skirt. Glue the reverse image to the other side and trim again.

3. Highlight selected features, such as the folds in the bodice or the halo, by brushing on embellishing adhesive followed by embossing powder and tiny glass beads. Shake off the excess powder and melt the powder that remains with a heat tool. Let dry.

4. Use the template to mark two wings on metal foil and cut out. Lay the wings in mirror image on newspaper or another padded surface. Emboss the wings by drawing spiral designs on them with a dull pencil or other blunt tool. Hot-glue the wings to the angel's shoulders with the embossing raised toward the outside.

5. Fit a piece of fabric around the torso to fashion a skirt. This angel's skirt is made from antique kimono fabric. It should fit like an isosceles triangle, with a single seam down the back. Slide the skirt onto the torso, and secure with fabric glue or a few hidden stitches.

6. Pierce a hole at the base of the neck with a pin, and insert metallic thread to create a hanging loop. Tie another piece of thread around the waist as a finishing touch.

Artist: Mary Ann Hall

Artist: Barbara Carlton Evans

Marina, Dancing Angel

You don't have to be a dancing fool to fall in love with Marina, whose Italian name means "belonging to the sea." With her funky copper wings, shimmering shell dress, and up-flung wire arms, she's got more to offer than just groovy dance-floor moves. And her splashy, sponge-painted background will add a lively tone of color to any room. Call her a celebrator of life, and give her to a friend who inspires you.

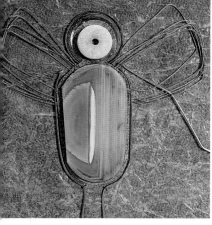

A variation

VARIATIONS *Since this project relies on natural materials, each angel will be different. Stay flexible, look through your stash, and use whatever catches your fancy. The Rock Dancer Angel (inset) has an agate slice body and bone-bead head. His halo is a rusted metal circle.*

MATERIALS
FOR 4" × 7" (10 CM × 18 CM) ANGEL

- 2 seashells for head and body
- 24- and 28-gauge copper wire
- thin copper sheet
- 8" × 10" (20 cm × 25 cm) mat board
- 8" × 10" (20 cm × 25 cm) precut mat with oval opening
- 5" × 7" (13 cm × 18 cm) art paper
- tissue paper
- acrylic paints, including metallic
- acrylic varnish
- epoxy or strong adhesive (this artist used E6000)
- natural sponge
- small jeweler's pliers
- general craft supplies

1. To prepare the background, sponge-paint the mat board and the oval mat, using several colors of paint and at least one metallic. Sponge on very light layers until you get an effect that pleases you. Paint the art paper in the same way. Set all aside to dry.

2. Cut a sheet of tissue paper about 1" (3 cm) larger than the mat board all around. Wad it into a ball, and then smooth it out flat. Brush varnish on the surface of the mat board, immediately lay the tissue paper on top, and smooth it down using a paintbrush and more varnish.

3. To make the body, glue the head and body shells to the art paper with epoxy and let dry. Trim the paper to within $\frac{1}{16}$" (2 mm) of the shells.

4. Shape 24-gauge wire into two wings, using your fingers and small jeweler's pliers. Place them on a piece of solid, flat metal, and gently hammer flat. Wrap the flattened wings with 28-gauge wire, criss-crossing back and forth.

5. Place the oval mat on the mat board. Position the wings and body in the opening. Cut and shape a little skirt from the copper sheet. Remove all the pieces, maintaining the arrangement. Glue them back into position one by one.

6. Cut arms and legs from the 24-gauge wire, shape as desired, and hammer flat. Position the limbs on the collage. To anchor them in place, pierce pairs of tiny holes through the mat board on either side of the limb. Cut a short length of 28-gauge wire, bend it into a hairpin shape, and insert the ends down through the holes. On the underside, pull the wires tight, twist the ends together, and splay flat. To prevent tarnishing, add a coat of varnish when the angel is finished.

Who better to sing in the celestial chorus than the King of Rock 'n Roll? Simple to make and fun to dress in a fashionably hip ensemble, he's one "hunka, hunka burning" angel. Here he's looking his sleekest best, but if the older Las Vegas Elvis appeals to you (as he does to impersonators around the globe), just "plump up" the template, choose a photo with bushy sideburns, and go crazy with those rhinestones.

Heavenly Muse

MATERIALS
FOR 8" (20 CM) ANGEL

- 1 sheet balsa wood, ⅛" (3 mm) thick
- photo image of of Elvis Presley
- two different patterned papers
- narrow metallic ribbon
- seed beads
- rhinestones
- large gold button
- acrylic paints in assorted colors
- matte decoupage medium
- craft glue
- general craft supplies
- templates A, B, and C (page 118)

TIP *If your Elvis head faces the wrong direction, simply flop the body and jacket templates before marking the pieces.*

1. Cut out your Elvis Presley head (the head shown is from an old calendar). Position template A and the head cutout together on the balsa wood, and trace all around. Also trace around template B. Cut out both pieces with a craft knife. Go over the cutting line gently, a few times, to avoid splitting the fragile wood. Be sure all lines have been cut clear through before trying to extract the pieces.

2. Paint the body and wings, including the edges and backs, in the colors of your choice. Let dry.

3. Cut a small square of white paper to use as a shirt, and trim it to suggest a neckline. Brush decoupage medium on the back of the white piece and glue it to the body. Use template C to mark the jacket on patterned paper, and cut out. Decoupage the jacket and head to the body. Let dry.

4. Use a fine-tip permanent black marker to draw in the sleeves, lapels, and other defining lines on the jacket and pants. Blacken the lapels and shoes. Apply decoupage medium to all the paint and paper surfaces and let dry. Add more coats if desired.

5. Glue on seed beads for the shirt buttons and rhinestones or other jewels for the jacket buttons. Add a ribbon bow at the neck for a tie.

6. Trace template B on the second patterned paper. Cut out ¼" (5 mm) inside the marked line. Decoupage the cutout to the wooden wing, leaving a visible painted border all around it. Let dry. Glue the wings to the back of the body. Seal the visible areas of the wings with decoupage medium. For a halo, glue a gold button to the back of Elvis's head in the manner of a medieval painting.

7. To display the Heavenly Muse, attach a hanger to the back or a hanging loop at the top, or simply prop him up.

VARIATIONS *Elvis doesn't rock your world? Make a template from any photo and follow the same basic techniques for an inspired homage to the celebrity of your choice.*

Artist: Holly Harrison

Artist: Michelle Locke

Ballerina Angel

You may already have an angel at home who dreams of being a ballerina. Here's her perfect

companion. Floating in a tutu made of iridescent fabric teardrops, this dancer bestows a

blessing on every recital. An easy-to-master technique of wrapping padded wire in strips of

cloth is the secret behind her long and lovely limbs.

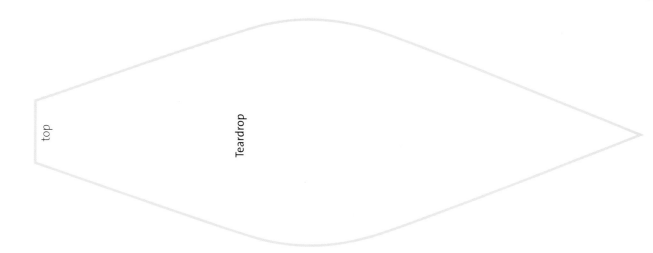

top

Teardrop

MATERIALS
FOR 12" (30 CM) ANGEL

- 1 yard (.9 m) white fabric
- ½ yard (.5 m) iridescent fabric
- ½ yard (.5 m) tulle
- scrap of gold fabric
- 1½ yards (1.4 m) 2"-wide (5 cm) iridescent ribbon
- 24" (61 cm) ½"-wide (1 cm) iridescent ribbon
- 16" (41 cm) fringe (for hair)
- embroidery floss
- assorted beads and trims for embellishment
- glitter
- 20-gauge cloth-covered stem wire
- 1 yard (.9 m) fat piping
- fiberfill
- fabric stiffener
- general sewing supplies
- template (this page)

VARIATIONS *This doll is versatile, and simple changes can create a whole new personality. Use different fabrics and embellishments to create an international dance troupe.*

1. For the head, cut a 7" (18 cm) circle of white fabric. Put a little fiberfill in the center, gather the fabric around it, and secure with a rubber band.

2. Cut several 1½"-wide (4 cm) strips of white fabric, at least 12" (30 cm) long. From the fat piping, cut a 4" (10 cm) torso, an 11" (28 cm) arm piece, and a 19" (48 cm) leg piece. Feed a piece of cloth-covered wire through each one and trim off excess. Center the arm piece on the torso about ½" (1 cm) from top and bind together with a strip of white fabric. Attach the leg piece at the other end in the same way.

3. Place the head on the neck and begin wrapping the strips around the neck, continuing down the torso to the arms and legs. Once the connecting joints of the body and head feel solid, secure the final strip with a few hand stitches.

4. Attach fringe to the doll's head for hair, starting at the nape of the neck and wrapping in a spiral until the head is covered. Glue or hand-sew as you go.

5. Neatly bind each arm and leg with cloth strips, starting at the hand or foot and ending at the body. Pin the end in place. Once all the limbs are wrapped, remove the pins, and bind the torso. Hand-stitch the final strip in place.

6. For the wing armature, bend the cloth-covered wire in half, open slightly, then bend again about 3½" (9 cm) from the center on each side. Bring the ends of the wire back to the center, forming a rounded wing on each side. Bind the ends to the center with embroidery floss. Flatten the armature, fold the gold fabric around it, and trim both layers ½" beyond the wire. Saturate the gold wing fabric with fabric stiffener, drape it over the wire frame, and press the edges together. Sprinkle the wings with glitter. Let dry. Shape the wings as desired. Attach them to the body by wrapping and securing them with a cloth strip.

7. Use the template to mark fifteen teardrops on iridescent fabric and thirty teardrops on tulle. Cut out all the pieces. Starting at the middle, sew the teardrops to the iridescent ribbon in overlapping layers, with the tulle as the underskirt, until the "waistband" is 4" to 5" (10 cm to 13 cm) long. Tie the skirt around the doll's waist and trim off the excess ribbon. For the bodice, wrap the 2" (5 cm) ribbon around the torso and secure below the skirt. Embellish your angel with jewels and beads as desired.

Real Woman Angels

If your best pal is frustrated in her diet yet again, give her some encouragement with an

angel who revels in her womanliness. With their luscious curves, siren charms, and fabulous

wardrobe, these two aren't about to be outclassed by any scrawny starlet wanna-be. As a

reminder that beauty comes in many forms, they'll keep the women in your life smiling for

a long time to come.

Artist: Barbara Carleton Evans

MATERIALS

FOR EACH 6" (15 CM) ANGEL

- two 11" × 11" (28 cm × 28 cm) squares of tightly woven fabric, such as silk broadcloth, cotton, or linen
- good-quality fiberfill that will stuff firmly
- fabric dye or paint
- assorted fabric trims
- approximately 18" (46 cm) wire-edged ribbon or lace
- sewing machine
- general sewing supplies
- templates A and B (this page)

1. Place the fabric squares right sides together, place templates A and B on top, and trace the outlines.

2. Machine-stitch on the marked lines through both layers. Leave an opening in the body A below the underarm (between the dots); stitch the head B completely around. Trim away the excess fabric ⅛" (3 mm) beyond the stitching line, increasing to ¼" (5 mm) at the opening. Clip the curves.

3. Cut a small slit in the head through one layer of fabric only. Turn right side out, stuff the head firmly, and sew the slit closed. Turn the body right side out through its opening. Sew the head to the upper part of the neck. Stuff the body, making the neck and limbs extra firm. Close the side opening using a ladder stitch.

4. Paint or dye the doll body and add facial features as desired.

5. To make the clothing and turbans, wrap various trims around the body and head and hand-sew them into place. For wings, tie wide wire-edged ribbon or lace into a bow, or cut a shorter length and crimp it in the middle. Hand-sew the wings to the angel's back, then bend and shape them as desired.

TIPS *A hanging cord may be sewn to the top of the head before you style the turban. If using fabric dye for the body, be sure it is compatible with the fabric you have chosen. Try paint with a slight shimmer alongside glitzy clothes for a dazzling effect. Using several trims to make the clothes will give the angel a lush, rich look.*

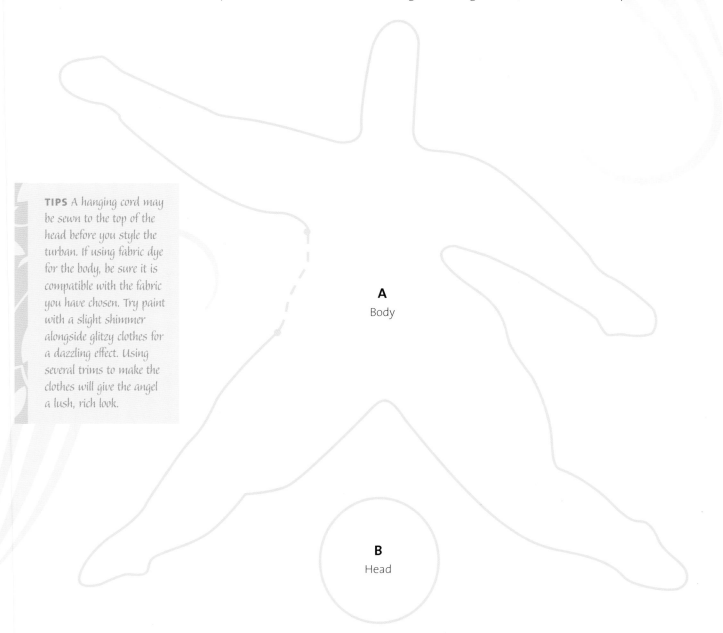

A
Body

B
Head

Artist: Sue Eyet

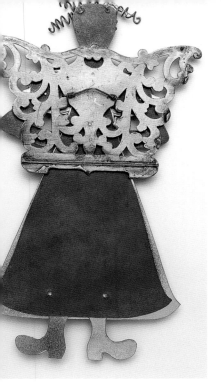

View from back

Friendship Angel

The Friendship Angel is more than just a friendly face—like Dorothy's pal, Tin Man, she carries a warm and generous heart within her metal chest. Don't let an unfamiliarity with the riveting technique put you off from this rewarding project. A little practice will help you master it, and in no time, you'll have assembled a host of new friends.

MATERIALS
FOR 7 1/2" (19 CM) ANGEL

- copper roof flashing
- large cookie or popcorn can
- 36-gauge aluminum tooling foil
- 20-gauge sterling silver wire
- 18-gauge copper wire
- 28-gauge brass wire
- seed beads
- star beads
- crystal beads
- double-coated tape (narrow tape on a dispenser works best)
- small anvil
- floral shears
- needle-nose pliers
- riveting jig (see page 17)
- small handheld drill with #65 bit (this artist used a Dremel tool)
- can opener
- patterns A–H (pages 78–79)

1. Make a riveting jig and rivets, as described on page 17.

2. To prepare recycled tin, remove the bottom from the cookie can, using a can opener that removes the entire end, including the rim. Carefully cut along the seam with floral shears and hammer flat.

3. Trace patterns A–H on tracing paper. Use rubber cement to affix tracings A, B1, and B2 to the copper flashing; C, D, E, and F to the reduced tin (the colorful side of popcorn/cookie can); G to the silver tin (the interior surface of the can); and H to the aluminum tooling foil. Using a dull pencil, mark a curlicue pattern on the H wings. [Note: The artist used a found object, salvaged from an old planter, to make the wings shown. These patterns are the artist's adaptation.]

4. Using floral shears, cut away the bulk of the waste metal around the pieces. Follow up with a closer, more detailed cutting, taking care to prevent burrs. Peel away the tracing paper, rub off the rubber cement, and hammer flat as needed.

5. Test-fit arm pieces B1 and B2 on the body A, overlapping to the dash lines indicated on the arm patterns. Using a #65 bit, drill rivet holes through both layers as marked. To attach the arms, line up the pieces, insert a rivet at each join, and turn the assembly over onto the flat surface of a small anvil. Press down at each join and clip away the excess wire with diagonal wire cutters, leaving about 1/16" (1 mm) of the rivet extending. Complete the riveting by gently tapping the extruding end with a hammer until flat, but not so tight that the arms cannot rotate freely.

TIP *Prior to starting this angel, make Dieter's Delight (page 14) and Sugar Shell Angel (page 17) to develop your metalworking skills.*

VARIATIONS *Because this angel relies on the use of found objects, you can vary her as much or as little as you wish.*

6. Drill the head and wrist holes as marked. Attach the leg piece C to the body with double-coated tape, drill two holes through both layers, and rivet in place. Layer and tape the clothing pieces D, E, and F to the body. Drill four holes down the front of the sweater and two holes on the collar (move the arms clear as needed), and rivet together. Tape wing piece H to piece G, drill a hole at each wing tip (four holes total), and rivet together. Drill the two remaining holes shown on the pattern if you wish to add a hanger. Tape the wings to the back of the body. Drill two holes, one at the center collar and one at the center waist, through all layers. Rivet the layers together.

7. Draw a face on the head with a fine-point permanent marker. For hair, cut two 4" (10 cm) pieces of 18-gauge copper wire. Wind each piece around a slender dowel (the artist used the ink cartridge of a ballpoint pen). Remove the coiled wire and stretch it slightly for curls. Crisscross one coiled length over the other, bind the join with brass wire, and clip off the excess. Use short pieces of brass wire to attach the copper curls to the holes in the head. Additional wire may be strung with seed beads to make a hair ribbon.

8. To join the hands, cut a 6" (15 cm) length of brass wire. Fold in half, string on a seed bead, and slide it down to the fold. Pass both wire ends through a hand hole, from back to front, until the seed bead catches. String several more seed beads onto both wires and slide them against the hand. Repeat for the second hand. Slip all four ends through a larger bead. Divide the strands, and resume stringing each double strand with seed beads, crystal beads, and star beads. To end off, separate the strands and curl each end individually with needle-nose pliers.

9. To add a hanger, thread 18-gauge copper wire through the two extra wing holes drilled in step 6. Slide the wire between the angel's neck and wings. Use needle-nose pliers to twist the wire ends together at the center back. Twist again ½" (1 cm) away, and open the space between the two twists into a circle. Clip off the excess.

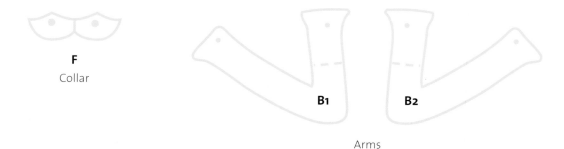

F
Collar

B1   **B2**

Arms

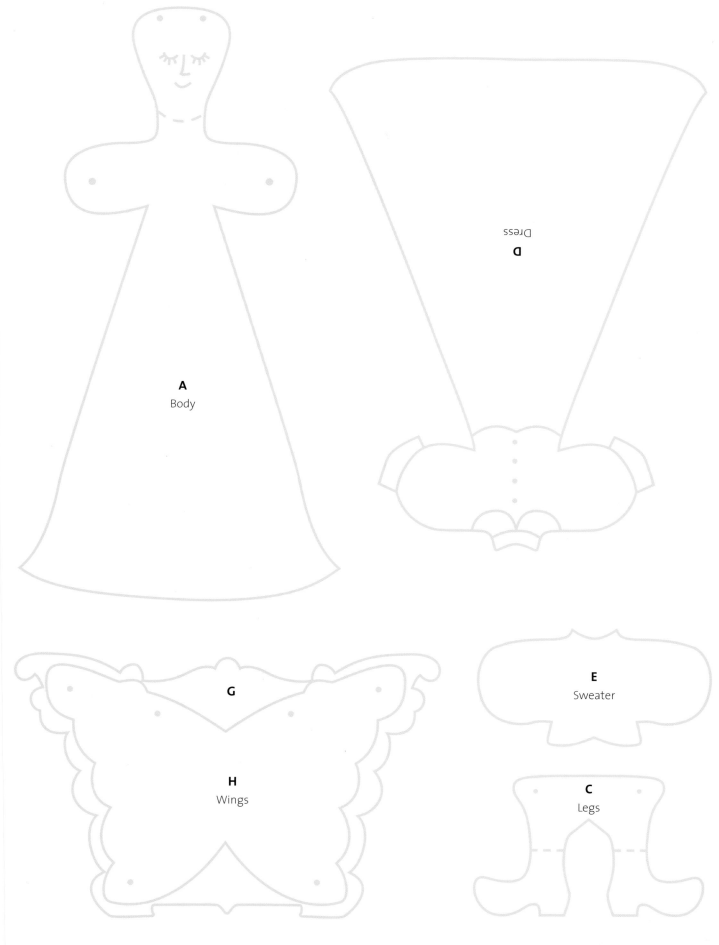

A
Body

D
Dress

G

H
Wings

E
Sweater

C
Legs

Angel of Good Fortune

They say good fortune comes from above, which is exactly where this angel makes her

home. In her colorful shadow box decorated with Mexican *milagros*, she's a powerful ally to

have in your corner. Hang the Angel of Good Fortune in the room that's the heart of your

home, and let her work her magic for you and your family.

MATERIALS
FOR 4" (10 CM) ANGEL IN 10" × 7" (25 CM × 18 CM) BOX

- 10" × 7" (25 cm × 18 cm) wooden shadow box with wide border frame
- 4" (10 cm) wooden heart cutout
- bottle cap
- colorful fabric scraps, including yellow
- 9 *milagros* (Mexican miracle charms) and small nails
- rhinestones
- glitter in red and gold
- 36- or 24-gauge copper wire
- gold vellum
- raffia
- yarn for hair
- cotton balls
- sawtooth hanger
- fine-point black and colored markers
- acrylic paints in red, yellow, green, purple, blue, orange, and black
- spray gloss varnish
- water-based varnish
- epoxy or strong adhesive (this artist used E6000)
- hot-glue gun
- glue stick
- white craft glue
- hammer
- general craft/sewing supplies

1. Paint the interior of the shadow box purple. Paint the border frame green and yellow. For a faux-finish look, brush on one coat, then apply a lighter shade on top of it.

2. Paint the heart red, sprinkle with red glitter, and let dry. Use epoxy to glue the heart to the box interior. Paint yellow squiggles on each side of the heart with a liner brush; highlight with black and orange. Paint the edges of border frame red. Let dry completely. Seal with a coat of spray gloss varnish.

3. Cut a 1" (3 cm) circle and two mitten shapes from vellum. Using a fine-point black marker, draw a face on the circle and draw fingers and nails on the hands. Highlight with colored markers. Adhere the face inside the bottle cap with a glue stick. Run a bead of white glue around the rim, and sprinkle with gold glitter to frame the face.

4. Cut six 5" (13 cm) pieces of black yarn. Tie the strands together at the middle and unravel the ends to make wavy hair. Hot-glue the hair to the top of the bottle cap. Trim as desired.

5. Cut three 4" × 6" (10 cm × 15 cm) pieces of fabric, two yellow and one multicolored. Crimp and stitch one long edge of each yellow piece to make a fan-shaped skirt. Crimp and tie the third piece in the middle to make wings. Pull out a few rows of thread on all the pieces to fringe the edges.

6. To make the halo, bend the copper wire in a circle around the glue stick tube. Leave a straight handle for gluing, and clip off the excess.

7. Use epoxy to adhere the wings to the center of the red heart. Attach the halo and bottle-cap face. Glue on the two skirts below the face. Thread a *milagro* onto a piece of raffia and glue it around her neck. Cut a slit on either side of the dress and slip in the hands so they appear to be holding the *milagro*. Pull at the fibers in the cotton balls until they look like clouds, and hot-glue them to the box interior. Nail or glue the remaining *milagros* around the border of the box, and decorate with rhinestones and paint. Let dry overnight. Brush water-based varnish on the border frame to seal. Add a sawtooth picture hanger to the back for hanging.

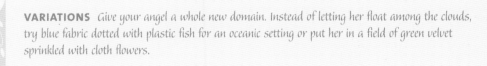

VARIATIONS *Give your angel a whole new domain. Instead of letting her float among the clouds, try blue fabric dotted with plastic fish for an oceanic setting or put her in a field of green velvet sprinkled with cloth flowers.*

Artist: Kathy Cano-Murillo

Bring some joy into a loved one's life (or even your own) with this angel crafted from recycled wire and bits of cloth. Not only is she easy on the eyes in her pretty pink-and-white organza dress, she's fun to make. Dress her up in silks, dress her down in earthy burlap, she still remains the same happy being at heart.

Happiness Angel

MATERIALS
FOR 5 1/2" (14 CM) ANGEL

- 16- or 18-gauge rusty wire for body
- 20-gauge rusty wire for arms
- thick ecru plastic-coated wire for wings
- 26-gauge craft wire
- monofilament
- 12" × 12" (30 × 30 cm) sheer ivory or off-white organza or lace
- small artificial flowers (roses, forget-me-nots, etc.)
- 1/4" (5 mm) crystal bead
- 12" (30 cm) 1/4"-wide (5 mm) rose-colored satin ribbon
- fine silver glitter
- green dried florist's moss
- quick-tack no-run craft glue
- hot-glue gun
- wire cutters
- needle-nose and regular pliers
- general craft/sewing supplies

1. To make the armature, cut one 12" (30 cm) length from each wire (except the 26-gauge wire). Bend the heavier rusty wire around a fat pencil or wooden dowel to shape a head approximately 1/2" (1 cm) in diameter. Twist two or three times to form a neck. Remove the pencil. To add the arms and wings, hold the two remaining wires against the base of the neck. Bind the join with 26-gauge wire, wrapping it in an X pattern until secure. Twist the wire ends together, snip off the excess, and crimp with pliers.

2. Cut each rusty wire "arm" to measure 2" to 3" (5 cm to 8 cm) long. Use needle-nose pliers to form small circles at the ends for hands. Cut each "wing" wire to measure 3" to 4" (8 cm to 10 cm) long, and bend into a spiral as shown. Cut the legs even.

3. Cut a piece of organza or lace for the skirt, making the waistband edge two to three times the skirt length. Hand-sew a loose running stitch along the waistband edge, pull tightly to gather, and test-fit on the armature. Hot-glue in place, with the opening at the back. Bind the waist tightly with 26-gauge wire. Conceal the wire and glue by wrapping pink ribbon around the torso and tying it in a bow at the back. Hot-glue flowers to the front waist. Tuck and glue in bits of green moss as desired.

4. Thread a length of monofilament through the head. Make a knot 1/2" (1 cm) above the head. String on the crystal bead for a halo, and secure with a second knot. Apply craft glue to the wings, head, and skirt as desired and sprinkle with glitter.

TIP *Use found and recycled fabrics, wire, and other materials whenever you can to give your angels an artisan look.*

Artist: Suzi Carson

Wheel attachment

Joy

Like a child with her first pair of roller skates, the angel named Joy delights in the simple things—a smile from a friend, new buds in the flower garden, a drawing made by the youngest family member. The featured angel is made of mud from the Mississippi River, but with simple modeling clay you can create a "holy roller" of your own.

MATERIALS
FOR 8" (20 CM) ANGEL

- clay*
- 8 white beads for wheels
- 16 small round gold beads
- doll's white dress
- doll stand
- acrylic paints in orange, white, black, and burnt umber
- matte acrylic varnish or polyurethane
- clay sculpting tools
- wire
- wire cutters
- skewer
- templates A–F (page 119)

*You can use any kind of clay for this project, but consider asking for self-drying clay at a craft store.

1. Condition your clay according to the manufacturer's directions. Roll a handful of clay and shape a ball head at one end. Sculpt a face on the ball and add clay for hair. With the angel facing you, pinch the bottom to shape the lower torso to match template A. Use a skewer to pierce two holes sideways through the body, as shown in template B, so that the arms and legs can be wired on later. Compare your work to templates A and B to further refine the shapes.

2. Roll out two small pieces of clay for the arms, shaping to match templates C and D. Pierce a hole at the top of each arm, from the side, for wiring. Make two legs to match templates E and F. Pierce a hole at the top of each leg, and put two holes through each foot, one at the front and one at the heel, for the wheels. Let all the clay pieces dry until hard (or fire them, if that is appropriate for your clay).

3. To assemble the angel, thread wire through the torso holes and around the arms and legs, twisting the ends to secure. For the skate wheels, cut a short length of wire, and loop one end. Slip on a gold bead, a white bead, and another gold bead, run the wire through a hole in the foot, and add three more beads in the same sequence on the opposite side (see photo inset). To secure, loop the other end close to the bead "wheels," and trim off the excess. Repeat for each set of wheels.

4. Use acrylic paints to color the angel as desired. If your clay is white, paint a base coat of orange, let it dry, and then add a coat of burnt umber to get a deep brown tone for the skin. Seal with a coat of matte acrylic varnish or polyurethane.

5. Dress the angel doll and add wings as desired. A friend of the artist made the dress that is shown using a commercial pattern; you might use a pattern, sew your own design, or purchase a ready-made doll dress. The wings can be purchased or sewn from gold fabric.

6. Paint decorative swirls on the doll stand. Let the stand dry overnight before using it to display your angel.

VARIATIONS *Don't limit yourself to making just one kind of angel. Joy can be young or old, black or white, gregarious or shy, depending on how you sculpt and paint her.*

Charity

Her sweet face attests to a kind nature, her simple muslin dress to unaffected ways—and

what could be more appropriate for an angel whose name is Charity? With her at your side

(or on your shelf or pillow or desk), you'll find yourself being a little more patient, a little more

giving, not to mention just a little happier.

View from back

MATERIALS
FOR 8" (20 CM) ANGEL

- ½ yard (.5 m) muslin
- 5" × 8" (13 cm × 20 cm) quilted muslin
- 2" (5 cm) grapevine wreath
- 4 satin rosebuds
- fabric marking pens or embroidery floss
- off-white and blue thread
- fiberfill
- pink chalk or blush
- coffee
- hot-glue gun
- general sewing supplies
- templates A–G (page 119)

Artist: Kathy Underwood

1. Fold the muslin in half, right side in. Using the templates, mark A and B once and C, D, E, and F twice. Cut out E and F on the marked lines. Cut the other pieces apart, but do not cut them out. Do not separate the layers. Also cut a 2½" × 18½" (6 cm × 47 cm) piece for the skirt.

2. Machine-stitch A, B, C, and D on the marked lines, leaving a small opening between the dots for turning. Trim the seam allowance to ⅛" (3 mm), more at the openings. Turn right side out, stuff firmly, and sew the openings closed.

3. Sculpt the fingers using a needle and a double strand of off-white thread. Draw the needle out at the base of the finger, loop the thread over the top of the hand, reinsert it, and draw through to the starting point, pulling up tightly. Repeat for the rest of the fingers and the toes. Sew the head, arms, and legs to the body.

4. Cut one E bodice in half along the fold line for the bodice backs. Sew the backs to the front, right sides together, along the shoulder seams. Hem the neckline and each wrist edge. Stitch the underarm and side seams and clip as indicated. Hem one long edge of the skirt. Gather the opposite edge, and join to the bodice. Stitch the skirt back seam, stopping 1" (3 cm) below the waist. Fold in the raw edges and topstitch. Turn right side out.

5. Stitch the pant pieces together from the crotch to the waist. Open up both sets, place them right sides together, and sew one side seam. Fold the waist edge ½" (1 cm) to the wrong side, and topstitch. Sew the other side seam. Hem each pant leg, then sew the inseam. Clip the curves, and turn right side out.

6. Cut the quilted muslin in half. Mark G on one piece. Place the pieces wrong sides together, and machine-stitch on the marked line through all the layers. Cut out the wings ⅛" (3 mm) beyond the stitching line. Tear several thin strips of plain muslin for hair. Dip the wings, hair, dress, and pants in coffee to dye them. Let dry. Press as desired.

7. Draw or embroider facial features as desired. Dress the doll, gathering the pants waist and dress wrist edges to fit. Stitch the back of the dress closed. Hot-glue the muslin hair strips, wreath halo, and wings in place. Add rosebuds to the bodice and back waist. Blush the fingers, toes, and cheeks.

VARIATIONS *Add a hanger for use as a tree ornament or fancy her up with a satin or silk dress.*

Artist: Neysa B. Neumann

An elegant design made of antique glass, the Blue Angel shines with quiet devotion. It may take some practice to acquire the skills necessary for crafting her, but like the state of mind she represents, your patience and dedication will be rewarded when she graces a window in your home.

Blue Angel

MATERIALS
FOR 9" (23 CM) ANGEL

- antique colored glass
- lead came and came stretcher
- soldering iron and 60/40 solder
- oleic acid for flux
- putty
- beeswax or soft modeling compound (this artist uses Play-Doh)
- pattern shears
- glass cutter
- cutting board and leading board (soft wood)
- small hammer
- glazing nails or horseshoe nails with flat sides
- piece of clear glass
- black ink
- brown kraft paper
- carbon paper
- wooden dowel
- cornstarch
- general craft supplies
- pattern (page 120)

TIP *Do not overheat the soldering iron as it will melt the lead. An iron that's too cool will not make a secure joint, so you might want to practice first.*

1. Layer three sheets of brown kraft paper, place the pattern on top, and interleave with carbon paper. Trace the lead design lines with a pencil. Number the pieces on each kraft paper pattern to correspond to the glass colors you will cut.

2. Set a piece of clear glass over one kraft paper pattern. Trace the lead lines of the pattern onto the glass, using an artist's watercolor brush and black ink.

3. Cut one kraft paper pattern apart along the design lines using the pattern shears. (Pattern shears have three blades. Cutting with them compensates for the extra space needed between the glass pieces for the heart of the lead.)

4. Use the glass cutter and cutting board to cut a piece of antique glass for each piece of the design, according to the color number. Place the cut pieces on top of the marked clear glass and adhere them with warm beeswax or modeling compound. Carefully lift the whole assembly and view it against a window or other light source to evaluate the color placement. When you are satisfied with the colors, proceed to step 5.

5. Tape the third kraft paper pattern to the leading board. Stretch and straighten the lead came, then cut it to match the outside line of the pattern. Beginning in the upper left of the design, transfer the pieces of antique glass from the clear glass plate into the outline of lead came. (Scrape off the beeswax as you proceed and save it for future projects.) Make sure the lead lines on the glazing board pattern are visible as you insert each piece of glass into the came. Tap lightly with a hammer to ensure a snug fit. Tap a glazing nail on the outside of the came into the board to press the came against the glass. Continue cutting and fitting until all the pieces are secured.

6. Heat the soldering iron. Use a cotton swab to dab each joint with oleic acid as you apply the solder. When all the joins are soldered, remove the glazing nails. Slide the entire board to the edge of your workbench, tilt the board at a 45° angle, and very carefully turn the piece over. Repeat the soldering process on this reverse side. Finish by pressing putty into the edges of the lead came, then smoothing the came with a wooden dowel. Remove any traces of putty with toothpicks.

7. Sprinkle cornstarch over each side. Brush with a soft bristle brush to clean the glass and remove any oil left by the putty.

If you're a person to whom words don't come easily but greeting cards seem too impersonal, keep reading. Made of everything from tulle and tin to paper and rubber stamp designs, feathers and silk to polymer clay and seed pearls, the angels in this chapter are special enough to rise to any occasion. It's just a matter of putting a little time into making them.

Moments in Time

Some projects are fairly simple, requiring only an hour or so to complete; others are quite complex and will necessitate a commitment of days. But whichever ones you undertake, you'll always end up with a unique offering for just about any occasion—a wedding, a birthday, a change in career. These colorful, glittery, and beaded angels beg to be given as gifts, to be wrapped in pretty paper and then happily unwrapped again.

So, don't just sit there reading. Grab your art supplies, set up a sturdy table, and start crafting.

Kiah, Angel of New Beginnings

Because her Nigerian name means "beginning of the seasons," Kiah is particularly fond of

special beginnings such as the birth of a baby, an engagement or wedding, or even the start

of a new career. She also likes to celebrate the changing seasons and can be filled with herbs

or dried flowers accordingly.

MATERIALS

FOR 7½" (19 CM) ANGEL

- three 9" × 12" (23 cm × 30 cm) pieces of tulle in contrasting colors
- ½ yard (.5 m) cotton fabric in a skin tone of your choice
- cheesecloth
- 1 yard (.9 m) metallic yarn to match tulle
- 2 velvet leaves, each 2½" (6 cm) long, for wings
- size 11 seed beads in four colors
- small bells and charms
- fiberfill
- herbs and/or spices
- Hot Foil Pen and foil
- colored pencils (see step 4)
- fabric pens in brown, black, and red
- beading needle
- black beading thread
- turning and stuffing tools such as hemostats
- general sewing supplies
- templates A–D, face pattern (page 94)

View from back

1. Fold the skin-tone fabric in half, right side in, and arrange templates A–C on top, observing the grain line on A. Using a pencil, trace A once and B and C twice, allowing at least ½" (1 cm) between pieces. Without unfolding the fabric, cut the pieces apart. Do not cut out.

2. Stitch pieces A, B, and C on the solid marked lines through both layers of fabric. For the head, stitch all around. For the arms, stitch down each side, tacking at the beginning and end of each line of stitching and leaving the top and bottom open. For the feet, leave the top open. Cut out all five pieces ³⁄₁₆" (4 mm) beyond the marked lines all around. Cut a slit in one of the head fabrics for turning. Clip the curves, turn the pieces right side out, and stuff with fiberfill. Set aside.

3. Layer the three tulle pieces right side up in the desired order. Trace around template D twice, to make two three-layer pieces. Cut out both pieces ½" (1 cm) beyond the marked line all around. Pin the arms and feet to one piece between the dots, edges matching. Lay the second piece facedown on top. Stitch down each side and across the bottom through all layers. Turn right side out. Fold the top edge to the inside. Topstitch to close the opening, and then continue topstitching all around the bag. Cut a slit through three layers at the top back edge. Thread three strands of the metallic yarn along the slit to close the sachet bag later.

4. Lay the cheesecloth over the face pattern and trace the features. Position the cheesecloth on the head and go over the markings with a brown pen. Remove the cheesecloth, and darken the markings on the head as needed. Shade the face with colored pencils, coloring the irises with two shades of brown and the lips with two shades of red. Blush the cheeks. With a cream or white pencil, lighten the forehead and one side of the nose and chin. Use a white gel roller for the whites of the eyes. Blacken the pupil with a black pen, and add a white highlight. Add a bit of white to the lower lip. Add black eyelashes and eyebrows.

5. For hair, thread a beading needle with 1 yard (.9 m) beading thread. Fasten the thread to the back of the head, and come out toward the front of the head at one side. String five black beads, a colored bead, and another black bead on the needle. Skipping the last black bead, pass the needle back through the colored bead and the five black beads and then back into her head. Pull snug. Continue working up the side of her head, cutting back to four black beads at the eye and temple area and three black beads across the crown. Work down the other side of the head to correspond. When done, sew the head to the front of the tulle bag.

6. Thread the beading needle with ½ yard (.5 m) beading thread. Fasten the thread to one upper arm at the seam. Thread enough seed beads to go from one arm seam to the other and then reattach the thread. Repeat, making four or five rows of beads to simulate bracelets high on each arm. Tie three strands of the metallic yarn around each arm to suggest hands. Attach charms to the ends.

7. Lay one leaf velvet side up. Place the foil, shiny side up, on top. Using the Hot Foil Pen, trace over the leaf veins, feeling for them as you go, to gild them with foil. Hand-sew the wings to the angel's back.

8. Fill the sachet bag with your choice of herbs and spices. Draw the closing threads and tie them in a bow at the back (see photo inset at left).

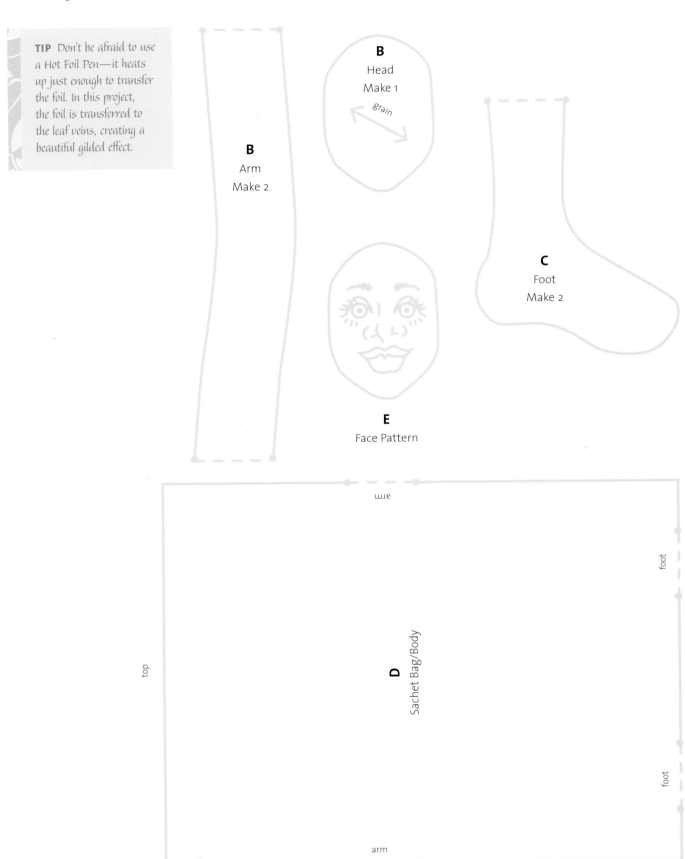

TIP Don't be afraid to use a Hot Foil Pen—it heats up just enough to transfer the foil. In this project, the foil is transferred to the leaf veins, creating a beautiful gilded effect.

B
Arm
Make 2

B
Head
Make 1
grain

C
Foot
Make 2

E
Face Pattern

D
Sachet Bag/Body

top

arm

foot

foot

arm

Artist: Barbara Carleton Evans

Who needs a dozen long-stemmed roses (that old cliché) when there's this charming Valentine Angel to be had? She's so in touch with her feelings that she literally has "love" written all over her. And with a little research on your part, she can say it in any language. Not just for sweet-hearts, she will happily grace the home of a much-loved grandma or grandpa, delighted parents, or a dear friend.

Valentine Angel

MATERIALS
FOR 10" (25 CM) ANGEL

- 12" × 16" (30 cm × 41 cm) thick red art paper
- paper heart shapes
- beads, feathers, and embellishments for headdress
- 2 bamboo skewers
- small wood plaque
- wooden block in an interesting shape
- thick white tacky glue (this artist used Aleene's Thick Designer Tacky Glue)
- 1/8" (3 mm) hole punch
- small handheld drill (this artist used a Dremel tool)
- general craft supplies
- templates A, B, and C (page 120)

1. Fold the art paper in half crosswise. Place templates A, B, and C on top, aligning A on the fold. Trace the outlines, and cut out. Punch out a tiny half-circle in A for the dress neck opening.

2. Cut one skewer into two 2¼" (6 cm) lengths for arms. Insert the other skewer up through the neck hole, for the head and neck. Open up the dress and apply a bead of glue along the skewer and the fold lines. Set the arm pieces in the folds. Fold back down and press gently until dry.

3. Glue the head ovals back-to-back to the neck skewer. Add hair, feathers, paper cutouts, and embellishments to create a headdress. Flat pieces, such as feathers, can be sandwiched in between the ovals.

4. Glue the wings pieces together back-to-back. Glue the wings to the angel's back. Glue heart-shaped paper cutouts to the dress and wings.

5. For the base, glue an interesting wood shape, such as a triangle or half-circle, to the small wood plaque and let dry. Drill a small hole through both pieces just large enough to hold the skewer tightly. Glue in place.

TIP If you do not have a heart–shaped hole punch, cut out the paper shapes by hand or buy heart–shaped jewels or charms. You can also cover her with flowers or anything else interesting out of your stash.

Instead of stringing popcorn and cranberries this year, why not make a pretty garland out of green, red, and white soda cans? A creative take on holiday decorating, this garland can be hung on a wall, wrapped around a column, or strung on your tree. Substitute other colors and types of metal to make a garland for a birthday, baby shower, or wedding reception—after all, angels are welcome guests at any celebration.

Artist: Laura McFadden

Angel Garland

MATERIALS
FOR 36" (91 CM) GARLAND

- about 20 empty soda cans in various colors
- 50 silver 9-mm jump rings
- tin snips
- heavy-duty gloves
- hole punch
- needle-nose pliers
- general craft supplies
- template (this page)

TIP *The cut metal is sharp, so do wear a pair of heavy-duty work gloves while cutting out the angel shapes.*

1. Wash out the empty soda cans, and let them dry upside down on a drain board or dish towels.

2. Using tin snips and starting at the opening, cut off the top of one can, including the rim, and discard. Cut along the seam until you reach the bottom. Cut off and discard the bottom. Open out the remaining piece into a flat rectangle.

3. Lay the rectangle printed side down. Place the angel template on top, and trace the outline with a fine-tip permanent marker. Cut out the angel using scissors or a craft knife. Punch holes at each end, as indicated. Repeat steps 2 and 3 for each can, or until you have enough angels for your desired garland length.

4. Link the angels together with silver jump rings. Use needle-nose pliers to open and close the rings.

Honor the youngest angel in the family by making a personalized ornament. The New Angel has a flexible design that works for boys and girls alike and is a handy way to recycle soda cans to boot. On those days when your youngster is acting anything but angelic, the ornament version of his better self will remind you that this too shall pass.

Artist: Laura McFadden

New Angel

1. Follow Angel Garland, step 1 (previous page).

2. Follow Angel Garland, step 2 (previous page) for both cans.

3. Lay the rectangles printed side down. Place templates A and B on top, and trace the outlines with a fine-tip permanent marker. Cut out each piece using scissors or a craft knife. Punch three holes in the torso and five holes in the skirt, as indicated. Turn the torso silver side up, and use a metal nail to score lines in the wings, as indicated.

4. To make a head, set the bottle cap, label side up, on a hard surface and smash it flat with a hammer. Use a hammer and nail to pierce a hole at the top and bottom of the cap. Cut out the face from your photograph and glue it to the cap. Run a bead of glue around the face, sprinkle with red glitter, and let dry for 1 hour. Shake off the excess glitter.

5. Link the head, torso, skirt, and feet together with silver jump rings, as shown. Use needle-nose pliers to open and close the rings.

VARIATIONS *Substitute photographs of other babies, family members, or friends to make everyone an angel! Please note: These angel figures are fragile and have sharp edges—they are not child-friendly.*

MATERIALS
FOR 8" (20 CM) ANGEL

- 2 empty soda cans
- photograph of baby
- bottle cap
- 2 silver feet *milagros* (Mexican miracle charms)
- 5 silver 9-mm jump rings
- red glitter
- craft glue
- tin snips
- heavy-duty gloves
- hole punch
- needle-nose pliers
- hammer and nail
- general craft supplies
- templates A and B (page 121)

The New Year's Angel ushers in the new by revamping fashions gone by: She's definitely vogueing in her mod pom-pom dress and sparkly wings. In fact, her dress cries out for a pair of white Nancy Sinatra walking boots. Retro appeal makes her a beguiling ambassador of the coming year's good tidings.

Artist: Cindy Gorder

New Year's Angel

MATERIALS
FOR 5" (13 CM) ANGEL

- 5" (13 cm) cloth doll body
- iridescent beads or pearls
- narrow white satin and eggshell sheer ribbons for hair
- iridescent ½" (1 cm) pom-poms
- 10 stems of wired pearls for wings (from a floral department)
- 10" × 6" (25 cm × 15 cm) iridescent cellophane
- wire for halo
- water-based decoupage medium
- pink permanent ink or fabric paint
- cool-melt glue gun with long, narrow tip
- wire cutters or nail clippers
- general craft supplies

1. Draw a face on the doll with a fine-tip permanent marker. Dab on pink cheeks with a cotton swab, using permanent ink or fabric paint. Use a small, flat paintbrush to apply decoupage medium to the cheeks, arms, and feet. Let dry.

2. Glue pom-poms all over the doll front and back for a fuzzy-sweater effect. Glue a bead or pearl onto each toe.

3. Glue or stitch strips or loops of narrow ribbon to the head. Trim and arrange for hair as desired.

4. Divide the stems of wired pearls into two groups, and glue them to the back of the angel for wings. Make lengthwise accordion folds in the iridescent cellophane. Crimp at the middle and secure with a bit of wire. Glue the cellophane piece to the angel, fluffing it out for a second layer of wings.

5. Fashion a halo from wire, and glue it to the angel's back.

 TIP Use a curling iron to gently shape the bangs.

Artist: *Cindy Gorder*

Being a heavenly messenger doesn't mean you don't want to look your best—at least not if you're Teen Angel (far right). With a fashionably sheer gown and a hairstyle that would inspire envy among the glamorous movie star crowd, she still manages to look angelic. She would make a most charming gift to celebrate a teen's first party or dance, a thirteenth birthday or sweet sixteen, and, for the young at heart, prom night or graduation.

Teen Angel

1. Draw a face on the doll body with a permanent marker. Dab on pink cheeks with a cotton swab, using permanent ink or fabric paint. Use a small, flat paintbrush to apply sparkle decoupage medium on the cheeks, arms, and feet. Let dry.

2. Apply a coat of white paint to the feather wings to tone down the color. Let dry. Follow with a coat of sparkle decoupage medium. Let dry.

3. Glue two strips of ¼" (5 mm) ribbon to the body for shoulder straps. Glue a 1" (3 cm) ribbon around the waist for an underskirt, concealing the strap ends. Cut the sheer ribbon into two 18" (46 cm) lengths. Hand-sew a running stitch along one long edge of each piece, and pull to gather. Arrange one piece around the waist for a skirt, adjusting the gathers to fit. Glue in place, overlapping the short ends at the back. Glue on the second ribbon skirt just above or below the first one.

4. Stitch or glue loops of the needlework fiber to the doll's head for hair. Trim and style as desired.

5. Glue two pom-poms to the doll front, and add pearls to her toes. Glue the feather wings to the back of the doll. Shape the wire into a halo, and glue it to the doll's back.

MATERIALS
FOR 5" (13 CM) ANGEL

- 5" (13 cm) cloth doll body
- multiple-ply iridescent needlework fiber for hair
- feather butterfly for wings
- 1 yard (.9 m) 1½"-wide (4 cm) sheer ribbon
- scraps of opaque ribbon in 1" (3 cm) and ¼" (5 mm) widths
- 2 iridescent pearls for feet
- two ½" (1 cm) iridescent pom-poms
- wire for halo
- water-based "sparkle finish" decoupage medium
- pink permanent ink or fabric paint
- white acrylic paint
- cool-melt glue gun with long, narrow tip (this artist suggests Beacon fabric adhesive as an alternative)
- general craft/sewing supplies

VARIATION *Every teen needs a pal. For Teen Angel's companion, follow the directions above, using white chenille yarn for the hair, 18-gauge silver wire wings, a gold cord halo, and a satin frock.*

On a day with so many potential disasters-in-waiting, a run-of-the-mill guardian angel may not be enough to safeguard the nervous bride and groom. The Wedding Angel, serene in her regal white gown, not only brings beauty and grace to the day, but will later serve as a lasting reminder of the couple's pledge to love, honor, and cherish one other.

View from back

Wedding Angel

MATERIALS
FOR 11" (28 CM) ANGEL

- porcelain head and hands; head shown is 2⅜" (6 cm)
- ¾ yard (.7 m) white fabric
- ½ yard (.5 m) white lace with scalloped edge for overlay
- 2 yards (1.8 m) 2½"-wide (6 cm) transparent gold wire-edged ribbon
- 1 yard (.9 m) 2"-wide (5 cm) white wire-edged ribbon
- 50" (127 cm) ⅛"-wide (3 mm) white wire-edged ribbon
- gold cord (for halo)
- miniature artificial flowers
- 9" (23 cm) Styrofoam cone
- two 6-mm chenille stems, each 12" (30 cm) long
- thin craft wire
- ¼" (5 mm) fusible tape
- fray-preventive medium
- craft glue
- hot-glue gun
- general craft/sewing supplies

1. Twist the chenille stems together to make one piece. Glue a porcelain hand to each end. Set aside to dry.

2. From the white fabric, cut one 20" × 25" (51 cm × 64 cm) piece for the dress and two 6" × 11" (15 cm × 28 cm) pieces for the sleeves. Seal the edges to prevent fraying.

3. Fold one long edge of each sleeve ¼" (5 mm) to the wrong side. Fuse in place, following the fusing tape manufacturer's instructions. Fold each sleeve in half, right side in, and fuse the short edges together. Turn right side out. Bend the chenille stem arm piece back on itself at the middle so that each arm is 4" (10 cm) long. Slip a sleeve over each arm, gather the loose shoulder edges around the arm piece at the middle, and glue the entire assembly under the porcelain shoulder blades and breastplate. Let dry.

4. Fold the dress rectangle in half lengthwise, right side out. At each end, fuse the short edges together. Hand-sew the fused edges together to make a tube. Turn the skirt right side out. Hand-gather the raw edge, fit the skirt on the cone, and draw the gathers closed, about 1" (3 cm) below the top of the cone. Tie off. Secure the skirt waist with craft glue.

Artist: Elizabeth A. Phillips

TIP *Use a pencil to open bows and to curl the narrow wire-edged ribbon.*

5. For a lace overlay, cut a 9" × 25" (23 cm × 64 cm) piece of lace, oriented so that the scalloping falls on a longer edge. Sew the short ends together, gather the raw edge, and fit on the cone as in step 4.

6. Hot-glue the head to the top of the cone, pushing the cone up into the breastplate for a secure hold. Glue the midpoint of the white ribbon to the back of the breastplate. Bring the ends over the shoulders to the front and secure at the angel's chest with thread or thin wire. Adjust the ribbon to hide the porcelain and dress seams, and glue in place. Glue on three miniature flowers to hide the thread.

7. For the wings, hold the wide gold ribbon 1" (3 cm) from the end and make a 10" (25 cm) loop. Make a second loop in the opposite direction, meeting back at the center. Continue back and forth until you have three loops on each side. Crimp the center, and bind with thin wire. Wind the remaining ribbon once around the wire binding, secure with hot glue, and trim off the excess. Glue the wings to the angel's back. Add some miniature flowers.

8. For the halo, cut a 4" (10 cm) length of gold cording. Glue the ends together to form a circle. Cut a 10" (25 cm) length of narrow wire-edged ribbon, tie it into a bow, and glue over the join. Hot-glue the halo to the angel's head, letting the ribbon streamers trail down (see photo inset on page 101). Cut the remaining narrow ribbon in half. Tie one piece at each wrist to shape the sleeves, and let the ends coil down. Glue a stemmed flower in one hand.

VARIATIONS *Leave off the lace overlay and substitute a colorful silk or satin fabric for the gown to make a Bridesmaid Angel—a fitting gift for your bridesmaids or a pretty centerpiece for the reception.*

Artist: Dawn Houser

You won't find an angel with a sweeter temperament than the Love Letters Angel, whose specialty is matters of the heart. With her pretty Asian face and multiple-language stamps, she communicates on an international scale—most appropriate for the universal sentiment she represents. A fitting gift for any time you want to show a special person how you feel: birthdays, Mother's Day, engagements, and, of course, Valentine's Day.

Love Letters Angel

MATERIALS
FOR 11½" (29 CM) ANGEL

- card stock in ecru and pink
- white paper doily
- 2 die-cut "Cornice Wings"
- white mini-grommets
- silver cord
- assorted rubber stamps (this artist used "Lin-Lin," "Winged Post Label," "Zebra Butterfly," "Lettre," "Lace Snippet," "Sprinkled Sky," and "Everyday")
- postmark rubber stamps (this artist used "Far Off Posts" set)
- alphabet rubber stamps (this artist used "Carved in Stone" alphabet set)
- ink pads in black, rose, and white
- embossing powder in white and silver
- heat embossing gun
- pink glitter product (this artist used Beadazzles)
- craft glue

1. Stamp "Lin-Lin" on ecru card stock in black ink and let dry. Cut out carefully, then lightly dab rose ink on her cheeks for blush.

2. Draw a gown shape in proportion to the head on the pink card stock, and cut out. Glue the paper doily on top and let dry. Trim the doily even with the gown edge all around. Stamp various images in a random fashion over the surface of the doily. Let dry.

3. To make the lace edge, stamp "Lace Snippet" in white ink continuously across a scrap of pink card stock. Emboss in white. Cut out the strip, trim it to fit across the lower edge of the gown, and glue in place. Carefully glue the head to the gown.

4. Rub white ink all over the die-cut wings to build up an antique white finish. Let dry. Position the wings on the angel, and punch four holes through all layers with a hole punch. Attach a white grommet at each hole to secure the layers. String the silver cord through the four holes in a crisscross fashion.

5. Stamp "Sprinkled Sky" in silver ink on the ecru card stock and emboss in silver. Cut out several individual stars from this piece and glue them to the hair, skirt, and wings. Let dry completely.

6. Run a bead of glue along the neckline and sprinkle with pink glitter. Lay the angel flat and let dry overnight.

VARIATIONS *Use this basic technique to make a variety of angels, substituting different stamps and ink colors as desired.*

Artist: Artist: Holly Harrison

The Celebration Angel loves good news. Invited to a birthday, graduation, or gala black-tie event, this cherub will add sparkle to any party. Contrary to her fancy appearance, she's made of simple materials: handfuls of beads, a Styrofoam ball and cone, and a little glue. Use her as a centerpiece or place setting, or decorate with a host of angels to multiply the joy.

Celebration Angel

MATERIALS

FOR 5" (13 CM) ANGEL

- 1 package of white 6-mm × 9-mm pony beads
- 1 package of white 2.1-mm seed beads
- 1 package of silver bugle beads
- 4-mm E beads in blue, orange, and gold
- 2.1-mm seed beads in red and gold
- 12" (30 cm) ½"-wide (1 cm) white decorative trim
- 16- and 26-gauge copper wire
- 3" (8 cm) Styrofoam cone
- 1" (3 cm) Styrofoam ball
- 12" × 12" (30 cm × 30 cm) black fabric
- beading needle
- black beading thread
- craft glue
- wire cutters
- general craft supplies

1. Draw the black fabric up around the cone, crimp at the top, and bind tightly with 26-gauge wire. Cut off the excess fabric close to the wire binding. Cover the ball the same way. Jam a short piece of 16-gauge wire partway into the ball head at the crimped end. Glue in place. Push the other end into the cone body.

2. Thread the beading needle and string on white pony beads to make a "bracelet" to fit around the bottom of the cone. Tack the bead bracelet to the cone with five or six stitches evenly spaced all around. Add two rounds of blue E beads and one round of orange E beads, tying off after each one.

3. Secure the thread at the back, and string on enough white seed beads for seven continuous wraps around the cone. Unwrap the strand, brush glue on the cone, rewrap, and tie off. Add a single round of orange E beads, as in step 2. Do another continuous round of white seed beads up to the neck. Add another blue round. Conceal the fabric at the shoulder and neck area with a continuous strand of gold seed beads.

4. For the wings, cut two 6" (15 cm) lengths of 16-gauge wire. Bend the wires in matching arcs. Pierce two holes in the angel with a nail and glue the wings in place. Make ten bead drops for each wing, and tie them to the wire arcs (see photo). Secure the knots with glue. Cover each arc with white trim.

5. For each eye, sew a small circle of white seed beads to the head. Add an orange E bead at the center for the pupil. For the bottom lip, sew on a loose line of six red seed beads; for the top lip, use eight beads. For a halo, sew a piece of white trim in a circle and slip it around her head like a headband. Finish with gold seed bead earrings.

VARIATIONS *Go all natural: Use wood or bone beads in varying shades to make the dress and wings, glue shells around the hem, and use a braid of dried grass or flowers to cover the wing wires.*

A spirit who seems to be reflecting back on gentler times, the Amazing Grace angel is the keeper of happy holiday memories. The photo transfer process used for her hands and face creates the effect of a hand-tinted engraving, while her gown of layered silk and metallic organza conjure an opulent mood. Perch this angel on a high shelf or on top of your tree where she can watch over the festivities.

Amazing Grace

MATERIALS

FOR 12" (30 CM) ANGEL

- face, hands, and skirt decoration (page 108)
- 4" × 12" × ¼" (10 cm × 30 cm × 5 mm) balsa wood
- ½ yard (.5 m) white silk fabric
- ½ yard (.5 m) metallic organza
- 1 yard (.9 m) ⅜"-wide (9 mm) sheer metallic gold ribbon
- feather wings from a dove ornament
- 1 package of 2" (5 cm) white feathers
- 18-gauge brass or steel wire
- gesso
- watercolors
- oil of wintergreen
- craft glue
- fabric glue
- burnishing tool
- wire cutters
- sewing machine
- general craft/sewing supplies
- patterns A–E (page 122)

1. Transfer patterns A, B, and C to balsa wood. Cut out the pieces with a craft knife, tapering each hand at the wrist. Paint the pieces on both sides with four coats of gesso and let dry. Sand lightly with fine-grit sandpaper until smooth.

2. Photocopy the face, hands, and skirt decoration at the indicated percentages. Cut out each piece, leaving a paper tab at the neck and wrists. Position the head and hands facedown on the balsa wood cutout. Tape down at the tabs, making sure that the tape does not cover any of the underlying image.

3. Apply oil of wintergreen to the back of each photocopy with a cotton swab. Rub the area with a burnishing tool or the back of a spoon to transfer the image to the wood. Carefully lift up a corner of the cutout to check your progress—the transfer will appear as the mirror image of the photocopy. Let dry.

4. Paint the face, hair, and hands with watercolors; add some color to the reverse side of the balsa wood too. Use a craft knife to cut the arms from the torso, as indicated on the pattern (they will be reattached after the figure is dressed). Glue the hands to the arms and set aside.

5. Transfer the dress decoration to the gown fabric, taping the fabric to the work surface for stability. Using patterns D and E, cut out two dresses and four sleeves (reverse two) from white silk. Also cut two dresses from metallic organza.

TIP *Make extra photocopies of the face and skirt decoration to practice the photo transfer technique beforehand. Too much pressure or too much oil of wintergreen can result in a blurred image. Photo transfers work best with natural fibers, so use silk or cotton for the angel's gown.*

Artist: Paula Grasdal

Amazing Grace, continued

VARIATIONS *Substitute a family member's face for the drawing by photocopying a personal photograph, or make the gown from elegant handmade paper instead of fabric.*

6. Place each organza gown on a silk gown, all pieces right side up. Secure the layers with a thin line of fabric glue at each shoulder. Fold the hem, neckline, and armhole edges to the wrong side and glue down. Place the layered gown pieces right sides together, organza sandwiched in between the silk. Glue or sew one shoulder seam. Sew one side seam ⅛" (3 mm) in from the edge, from the armhole to the bottom hem. Sew the other side seam from the waist down, and press the remainder ⅛" (3 mm) to the wrong side. Turn the dress right side out and press the seams.

7. Pull the dress over the angel's head. Reattach the balsa arms, securing with craft glue and a few strips of glue-coated fabric, applied like tape. Fold and glue the wrist edge of each sleeve. Place the sleeve pieces right sides together and sew or glue the side edges. Turn the sleeves right side out, iron flat, and pull over the arms. Glue the top edge of each sleeve to the torso. Glue the remaining side and shoulder seams of the gown.

8. Using craft glue, attach extra feathers to the wings. Glue the wings to the back of the dress, holding until the glue is set.

9. For a stand, score two grooves on the back of the balsa figure, as indicated on pattern A. Cut a 12" (30 cm) piece of wire. Bend the wire into U shape about 1" (3 cm) wide. Bend the ends to make an L shape. Glue the wire ends to the grooves, letting the U extend out behind the figure. Glue a piece of fabric over the wire ends to secure them further.

Face
Study for the head of Leda,
c. 1505-7, Leonardo Da Vinci
Photocopy at 125%

Hands
Photocopy at 90%

Skirt Decoration
Photocopy at 150%

Want to have the right angel for any occasion? With angel tags, it's easy. Made using a variety of stamping and embossing techniques, these ambassadors of good cheer will beautifully express your deepest sentiments. A terrific gift in and of themselves, they can also be used as tags for wrapped-up packages or as holiday ornaments. Make a dozen and hang them from a ribbon for a festive garland.

Artist: Dawn Houser

Occasional Angels

MATERIALS
FOR 5" (13 CM) TAG ANGEL (TOP RIGHT)

- angel rubber stamp (this artist used "Faith")
- background rubber stamp (this artist used "Harlequin's Pajamas")
- manila tag
- gold cord
- beads and trinkets
- white card stock
- ink pads in various colors for the background
- gold ink pad
- gold embossing powder
- heat embossing tool
- craft glue
- general craft supplies

1. Stamp the "Faith" angel on white card stock in gold ink. Immediately sprinkle with gold embossing powder, and shake off the excess. Heat-emboss. Carefully cut out the angel using scissors and set aside.

2. Dab the the various colored ink pads all over the manila tag and let dry.

3. Stamp "Harlequin's Pajamas" in gold ink all over the tag and let dry.

4. Glue the embossed angel to the tag. String the gold cord in the tag hole and tie beads on it. Be sure the affixed pieces are thoroughly dry before stringing them to hang.

VARIATION *Instead of gluing an angel to a tag, try using the tag itself as her body. To make the 7" (18 cm) angel (top left), stamp "Keeping Score" in black over the inked tag. Stamp a "Minnie" face and "Angel Wings" on card stock and color or emboss them as desired. Cut out the pieces and glue them to the tag as shown. Complete with a wire for hanging and beads.*

Golden Angel

The timeless beauty of ancient Greek and Roman statues was the inspiration for the Golden Angel, who stands proudly in a headless, armless stance. She's not an easy project to complete, but more than worth the effort. In her shimmering robes, made, surprisingly, of thin sheets of polymer clay, she will lend elegance to any holiday celebration.

Wing attachment

NOTE *This project was made on a pasta machine with seven settings; a #1 sheet is ³⁄₁₆" (4 mm) thick and a #4 sheet is ¹⁄₁₆" (2 mm) thick. Use the settings on your machine that come closest to these dimensions.*

MATERIALS
FOR 9½" (24 CM) ANGEL

- six 2-oz. (56 g) blocks Premo polymer clay in gold
- 2 oz. (.6 ml) Translucent Liquid Sculpey
- 10 ml FIMO gloss varnish
- 20- and 34-gauge silver-finish beading wire
- seventy 4-mm white freshwater pearls
- gel-type super glue
- white poster board
- corrugated cardboard
- aluminum foil
- plastic wrap or zip-type sandwich bags
- clay work surface*
- pasta machine
- tissue blade or craft knife
- ripple blade or rotary pastry cutter that makes a wavy line
- acrylic brayer at least 4" (10 cm) wide
- bamboo skewer
- metal palette knife
- snug-fitting latex medical gloves
- metal baking tray
- wire cutters
- needle-nose pliers
- ½" (1 cm) flat synthetic paint-brush
- general craft supplies
- templates A–E, wing pattern F (page 123)

* sheet of acrylic, marble pastry board, or thin flexible cutting board

1. Condition the clay by working it with your hands or rolling it through the pasta machine until soft and pliable. For the mica shift (steps 6–7), condition three blocks of clay ahead of time in half-block portions. Roll out sheets at #2 thickness, stack them between sheets of white paper, and set aside on plastic wrap for 4 to 6 hours to leach out some of the plasticizer. Remove the paper and store the clay in plastic wrap until needed. You'll use the remaining three blocks of unleached clay to build the armature (steps 3–5).

2. Use template A to cut a support cone from poster board. Roll the cone, and tape the seam overlap. Stand the cone on a piece of corrugated cardboard and tape down the base. Wad a 10" × 12" (25 × 30 cm) piece of aluminum foil into a champagne cork shape, about 2¼" (6 cm) long and 1¾" (5 cm) across the bulbous end, to support the angel's hips, waist, and rib cage. Poke a hole through the bulbous end with a skewer. Align the hole on the tip of the cone and push the "cork" down about 1" (3 cm) from the top. Secure with tape.

3. Using half a block of unleached conditioned clay, roll a snake to fit the base of the cone. Flatten it slightly with the brayer and fasten snugly around the base. Add the scraps to another half-block of clay, and roll out a #1 sheet. Lay template B on top and cut using a tissue blade. Pinch clay piece B along the short ends, to taper them, as you wrap it around the foil form from back to front; overlap the ends and stretch gently to ease the drape over the hips.

4. Cut three 4" × 12" (10 cm × 30 cm) pieces of foil. Fold each piece in half lengthwise three times to make a strip ½" (1 cm) wide. Cut the strips into two 4" (10 cm) and four 5½" (14 cm) pieces. Add your scraps from step 3 to a full block of clay. Roll out strips at #4 thickness that are wide enough to fold over and completely cover the six foil strips, with ³⁄₈" (9 mm) at each end.

5. Add the strips to the cone assembly, working from the base up (see photo inset below). The four longer strips form the skirt support, and the shorter strips, spaced 1" (3 cm) apart, are the shoulders. Trim off any excess at the waist, and indent each skirt support slightly for a bell shape. Put the entire assembly on a baking sheet. Bake 30 minutes at 265°F (129°C), allowing at least 3" (8 cm) clearance from the oven ceiling. Let cool completely.

Angel armature

6. "Mica shift" is a term used to describe the way certain metallic polymer clays can be manipulated to create shimmery, almost 3-D patterns. There are many methods. This project uses a flat layering technique and includes two of Pier Voulkos's "invisible canes": the "record" and the "snail." Use one block of leached clay (from step 1) to create the following canes and shapes. Roll all of the sheets at least six times, or until the clay is very shiny.

RECORD CANE: Roll half a block at #1 thickness into a 3" × 4" (8 cm × 10 cm) sheet. Taper one short edge and roll it up tightly into a thick log. Cut off a 1" (3 cm) piece and set it aside for the first cane. Roll and stretch the remaining log to about two-thirds the original diameter; cut off a 2" (5 cm) piece and set aside. Reduce again to half the previous diameter, and cut off a 2" piece. Let all canes rest before making very thin slices to apply to the patterned sheet.

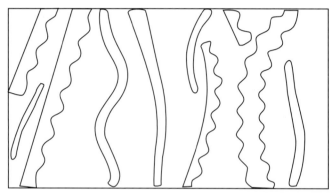

Layer One

Layer Two

Layer Three

SNAIL CANE: Cut 2" or 3" (5 cm or 8 cm) lengths of a record cane. Use the tissue blade to cut down through one piece diagonally. Roll each resulting wedge into a snail shape by starting from the thin end and keeping the shiny surface of the clay on the outside. Leave at original diameter or reduce as desired. Cut off thin slices as needed.

TWISTED STRIPS AND SNAKES: From a #1 sheet, cut several long strips about 3⁄16" (3⁄8 cm) wide. Twist each one loosely or tightly to make larger or smaller stripes. Leave some as is, roll some into smooth, striped snakes, and make some thinner.

FLAT SHAPES: Roll a sheet at #4 or #5 thickness, and cut out a variety of shapes and sizes. This project uses triangles and rectangles.

FLAT AND WAVY STRIPS: Roll a sheet at #4 or #5 thickness, and cut into long strips of varying widths up to 3⁄8" (9 mm). Use a straight or ripple blade, or cut your own edge designs.

7. Roll a half-block of clay at #1 thickness to a 3" × 4" (8 cm × 10 cm) sheet. For layer one, cover the sheet with a mixture of linear elements: long flat strips, wavy strips, striped snakes, etc. Roll with the brayer, pressing the pieces into the base sheet.

For layer two, apply a mixture of flat shapes and cane slices. Smooth slightly with the brayer. Roll the sheet through the pasta machine at #1. The first pass will buckle, so turn the piece 90° and roll through again. Repeat until the sheet flattens out. Then roll through at #2.

For layer three, apply additional shapes as desired, to fill in spaces or overlap other pieces. Smooth with the brayer. Roll through at #2, starting with the widest side if it fits. Roll through at #3, starting with the narrowest edge. Do the same at #4. Your final sheet should measure about 3¾" × 7" (10 cm × 18 cm). Make four sheets total.

TIPS *Never use tools or utensils with food after they have been used with polymer clay. Unbaked clay may ruin the finish on wood or painted surfaces—always keep it on a work surface or wrapped. Clean your tools and hands with rubbing alcohol. If the clay gets too warm and sticky as you are working, cool it in the refrigerator for a few minutes.*

8. Wear latex gloves to avoid fingerprints. Cut one skirt panel C from each mica shift sheet. Roll the scraps to a #4 thickness several times, or until lustrous gold. Cut four skirt trim D shapes. Ripple-cut the long edges.

9. Lay the skirt panels facedown, and rub Translucent Liquid Sculpey around the edges. Apply each panel to the armature, working from the base up and overlapping the support strips by ¼" (5 mm) at each edge. Let the extra panel width pouf out between the armature strips; gather in and pleat the fullness at the waistline. Before you smooth the waistline, slice off excess clay behind the pleat, in a hidden area, to avoid bulges. Once the waistline is adhered, refine the way the pleat falls to the base and work in ripples along the hem if desired. Where the hem does not flare out, press it gently against the base coil until it adheres. Apply the remaining three skirt panels in the same manner. Trim the top edge of the skirt even with the waistline.

10. Apply four skirt trim pieces to conceal the armature supports. Press gently, so that the seam lines do not show. Trim any excess.

11. Reroll all the scraps, make one more mica shift sheet, and cut one robe top E. Lift the robe with a skewer, drape it over the armature, and slide the skewer out. Press gently at the top of each shoulder, so the clay adheres without showing the support. Pinch below the waistline to flair out at the hips. Form a few loose ripples along the bottom edge. Rub a little Translucent Liquid Sculpey on the inside along the waistline, and adhere at the center back. Bring in the sides under the armhole a little more than halfway, so that the front pieces will overlap. Press at the waistline again at each side to adhere. Pinch out a pleat on either side of the center back and fold it toward the armhole, smoothing and pressing all along waistline to secure. Repeat for the front section. Use the skewer tip to get under the peplum ruffles and shape them.

12. Bake the entire assembly at 265°F (129°C) for 50 minutes. Cool completely. Wipe off the figure with a paper towel and rubbing alcohol. Apply varnish with a ½" (1 cm) brush. Let dry completely. Do not remove from the cardboard base.

13. Cut two 40" (102 cm) pieces of 20-gauge wire. Hold the wires together about 9" (23 cm) from one end, and twist for 1¼" (4 cm). Align the twisted section on the center line of the wing pattern F and tape down. Bend each long end to match the wing outlines on either side, taping as you go. When you reach the starting point, twist the short and long tails together once or twice and bend down in a lollipop shape; do not cut off. Remove the tape and pattern.

14. Cut a 36" (.9 m) piece of 34-gauge wire. Twist one end tightly a few times around the wing outline near the top. Then start zigzagging the wire across and down the wing, wrapping tightly around the wing outline each time it is reached. Nonserrated tweezers can help to pull the wire tight without kinking it. When you reach the bottom, start working your way back up, incorporating pearls into the design (thirty-five per wing) and making the pattern more random. Cut additional wire as needed.

15. To attach the wings, line up the top of the twisted section with the back of the neck opening, and bend to match the angel's figure. Hold the twisted section in place, wrap the two longer tails once around the waist from each side, and twist together at the back with needle-nose pliers. Continue wrapping both ends around the waist, ending at the back with little spirals. Wrap the shorter wires once around, ending off the same way. Dab gel-type super glue just below the neck opening; hold the twisted section in place until the glue sets (see photo inset at top of page 111). Gently bend the wings back slightly. Hold the angel at the waist and gently twist the base to remove the supports.

Patterns

Copy the patterns in this section on a photocopier, enlarging at the indicated percentage. To complete a half-pattern, make two photocopies in mirror image, and tape the two halves together. If the project calls for a template, trace the pattern outline onto template plastic and cut out the shape with scissors. For a sturdier template, mount the pattern onto heavy cardboard using spray adhesive and cut out with a craft knife.

Guardian Angel (shown on page 12)
Photocopy at 200%

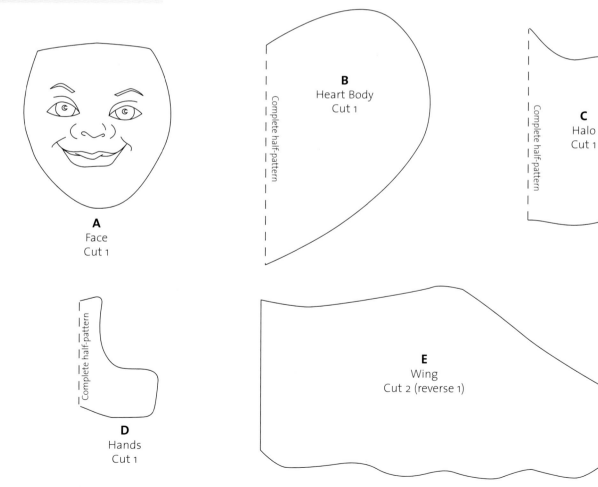

A
Face
Cut 1

Complete half-pattern

B
Heart Body
Cut 1

Complete half-pattern

C
Halo
Cut 1

Complete half-pattern

D
Hands
Cut 1

E
Wing
Cut 2 (reverse 1)

Home and Hearth Angel (shown on page 22)
Photocopy at 200%

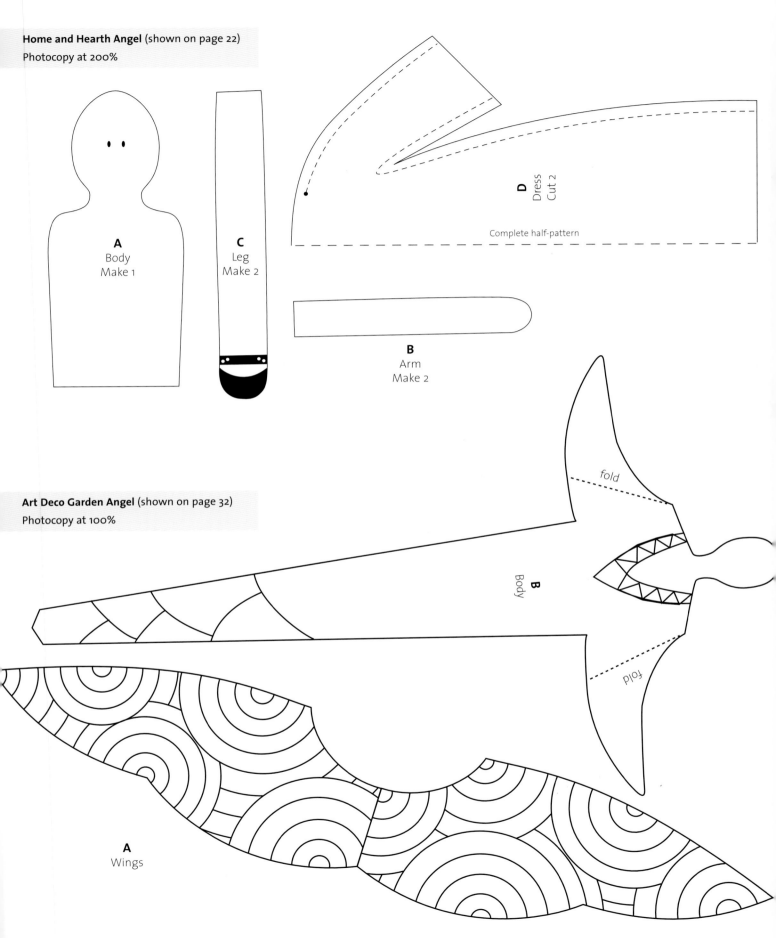

A
Body
Make 1

C
Leg
Make 2

D
Dress
Cut 2

Complete half-pattern

B
Arm
Make 2

Art Deco Garden Angel (shown on page 32)
Photocopy at 100%

fold

B
Body

fold

A
Wings

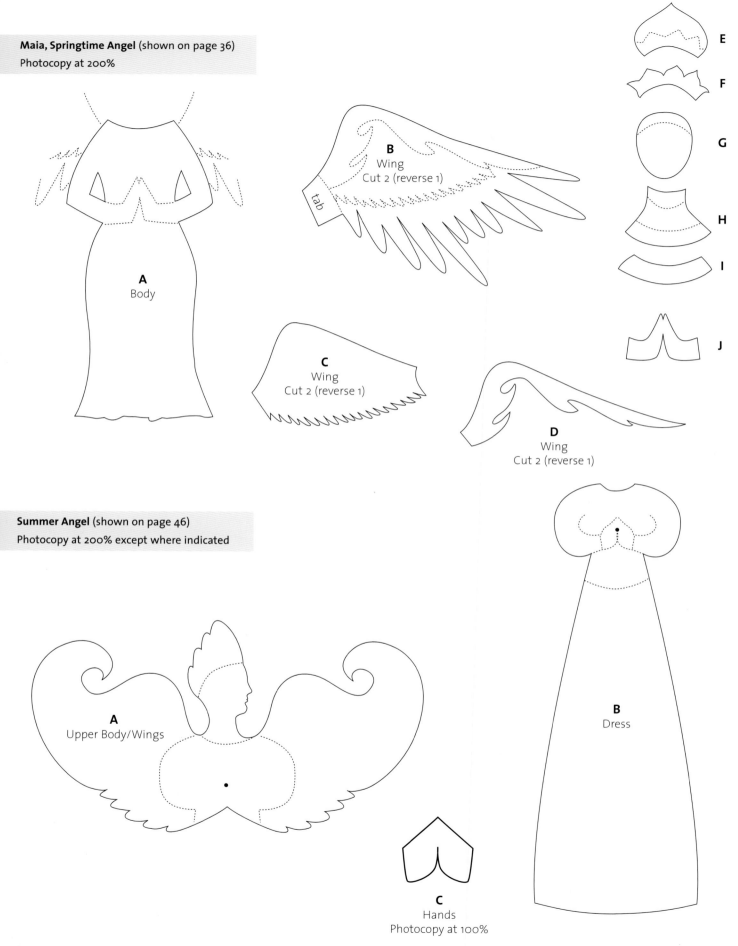

Maia, Springtime Angel (shown on page 36)
Photocopy at 200%

E

F

G

H

I

J

B
Wing
Cut 2 (reverse 1)

tab

A
Body

C
Wing
Cut 2 (reverse 1)

D
Wing
Cut 2 (reverse 1)

Summer Angel (shown on page 46)
Photocopy at 200% except where indicated

A
Upper Body/Wings

B
Dress

C
Hands
Photocopy at 100%

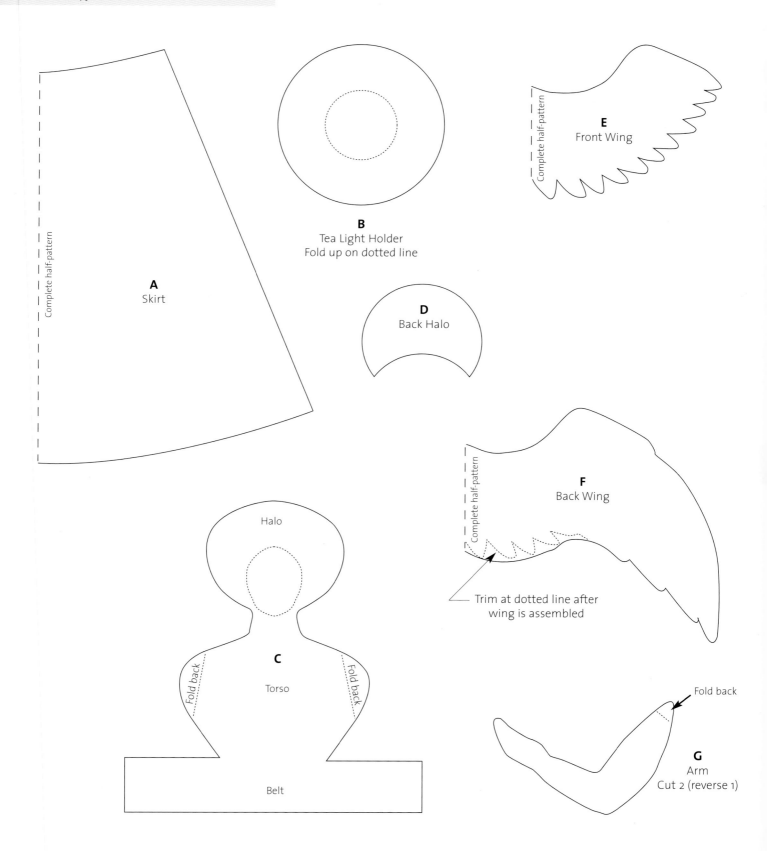

A
Skirt

Complete half-pattern

B
Tea Light Holder
Fold up on dotted line

E
Front Wing

Complete half-pattern

D
Back Halo

F
Back Wing

Complete half-pattern

Trim at dotted line after
wing is assembled

Halo

Fold back

C

Fold back

Torso

Belt

Fold back

G
Arm
Cut 2 (reverse 1)

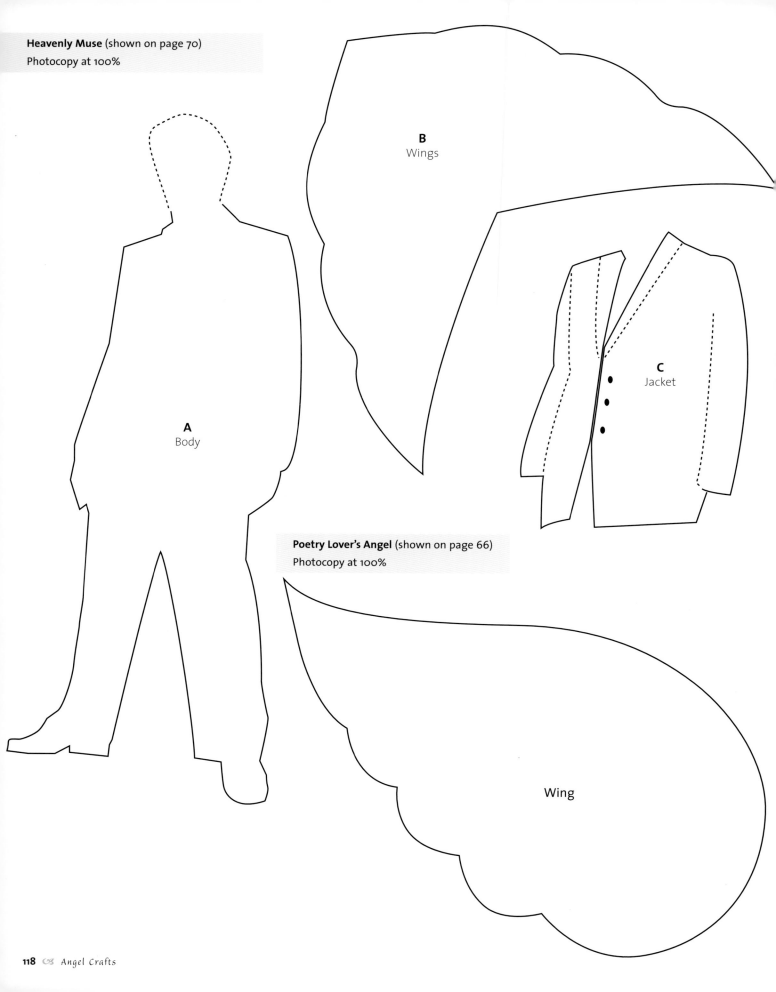

B
Wings

A
Body

C
Jacket

Poetry Lover's Angel (shown on page 66)
Photocopy at 100%

Wing

Joy (shown on page 84)
Photocopy at 200%

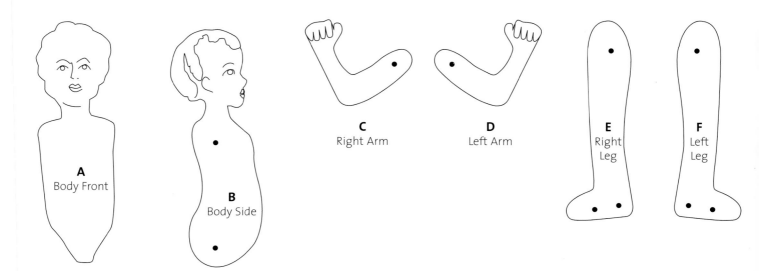

A
Body Front

B
Body Side

C
Right Arm

D
Left Arm

E
Right Leg

F
Left Leg

Charity (shown on page 86)
Photocopy at 200%

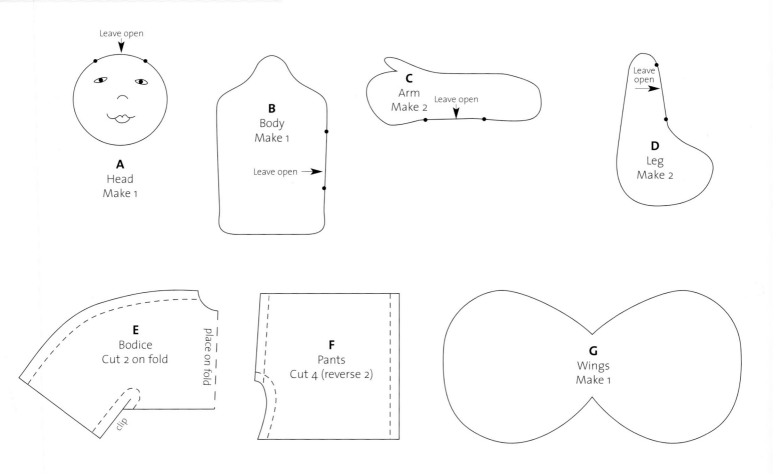

Leave open

A
Head
Make 1

B
Body
Make 1

Leave open

C
Arm
Make 2

Leave open

Leave open

D
Leg
Make 2

E
Bodice
Cut 2 on fold

place on fold

clip

F
Pants
Cut 4 (reverse 2)

G
Wings
Make 1

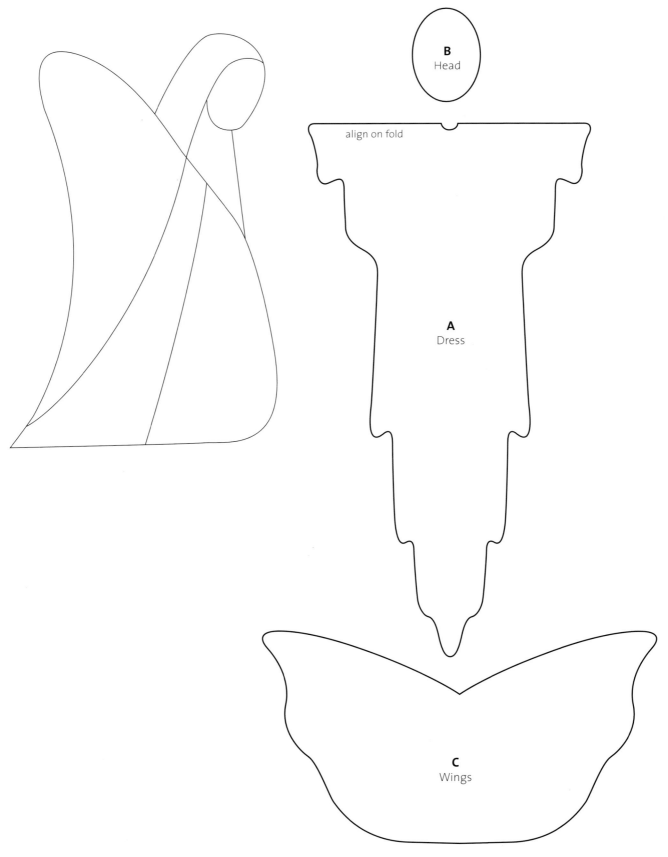

B
Head

align on fold

A
Dress

C
Wings

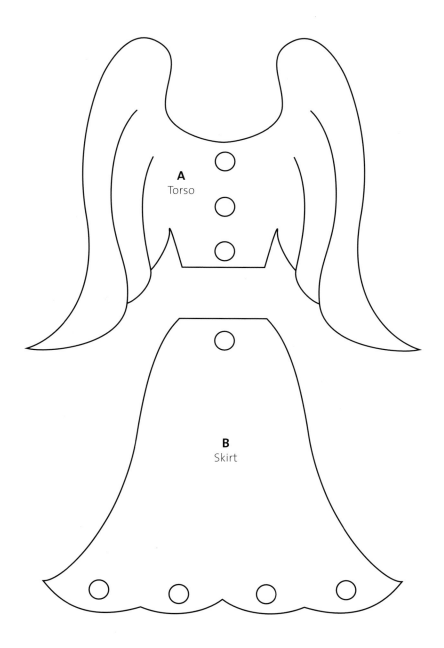

A

Torso

B

Skirt

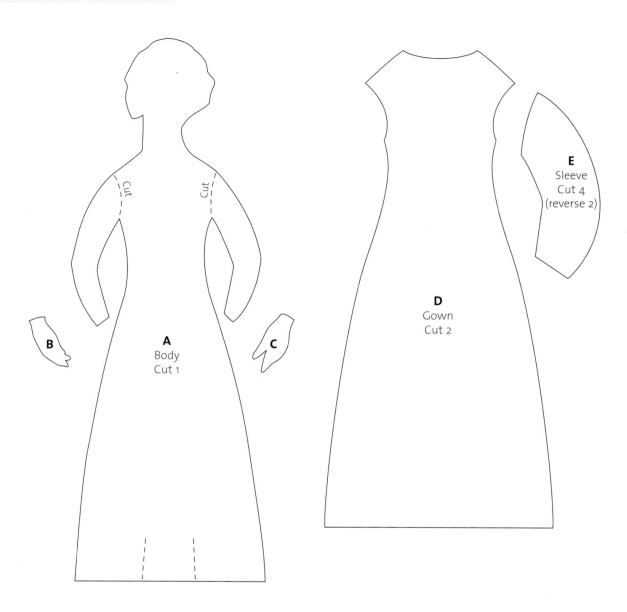

A
Body
Cut 1

B

C

Cut

Cut

D
Gown
Cut 2

E
Sleeve
Cut 4
(reverse 2)

Golden Angel (shown on page 110)
Photocopy at 200%

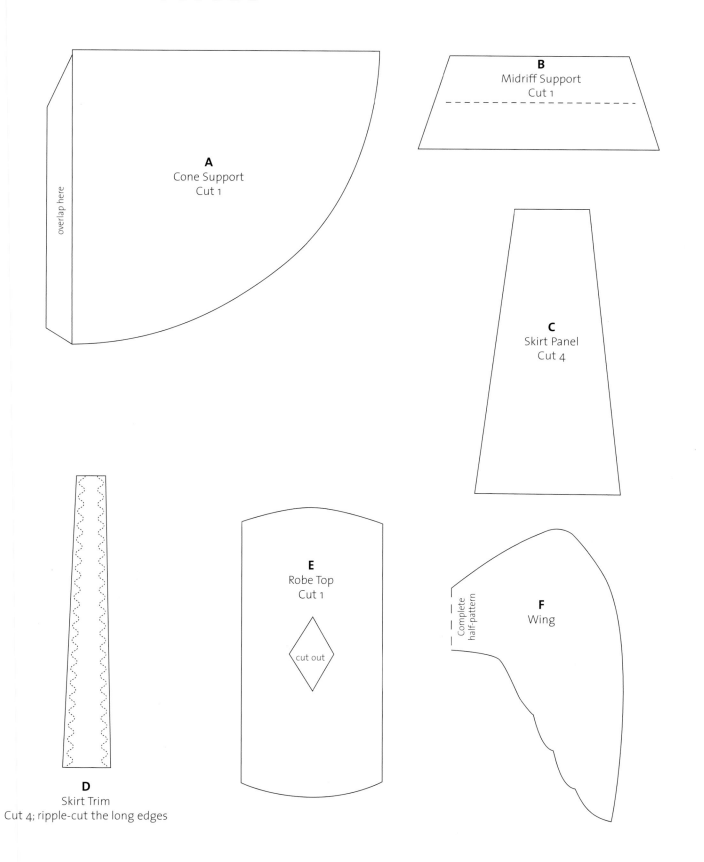

A
Cone Support
Cut 1

overlap here

B
Midriff Support
Cut 1

C
Skirt Panel
Cut 4

D
Skirt Trim
Cut 4; ripple-cut the long edges

E
Robe Top
Cut 1

cut out

F
Wing

Complete half-pattern

Artist Directory

Betty Auth

Auth-Antic Designs

14719 Earlswood Drive

Houston, TX 77083

Phone: (281) 879-0430

Fax: (281) 879-4310

bauth@houston.rr.com

Betty lives in Texas with her husband, John, and their two rescued dogs, Gypsy and Hobo. At Auth-Antic Designs, she creates and writes about wood burning, doll making, crazy quilting, and other creative pursuits. Her most recent book, Stamping Tricks for Scrapbooks, was released by Rockport Publishers in 2002.

Kathy Cano-Murillo

4223 W. Orchid Lane

Phoenix, AZ 85051

Phone: (623) 847-3750

kathymurillo@home.com

kathy.murillo@arizonarepublic.com

www.chicanofolkart.com

An Arizona native, Kathy is a feature writer, craft chemist, and mom who produces a line of Chicano pop art with her husband Patrick. Her writings, craft projects, and artwork can be viewed on her web site.

Suzi Carson

Flora Nevada Studio

4611 Maverick Avenue

Richmond, VA 23231

Phone: (804) 226-2324

A folk artist and toy and costume designer, Suzi creates spirited folk art that is carried in shops and galleries from New York to California. Her "Earth Angels" line includes such designs as holiday ornaments made from tin funnels, infant clothing made from dishcloths, and functional yard art.

Patti Medaris Culea

PMC Designs

9019 Stargaze Avenue

San Diego, CA 92129

Phone: (858) 484-5118

Fax: (858) 484-5122

pmcdolls@san.rr.com

Patti grew up in the Midwest as part of a creative family. Now a mother of two, she is a fiber artist who designs and makes beautiful cloth dolls and sells a full line of doll patterns. In demand as a teacher, she travels throughout the world.

Shirley DeLisi

P.O. Box 223023

Carmel, CA 93922

Phone: (831) 655-4769

Shirley is a lifelong doll artist. She creates dolls from the soul that hold her "childhood spirit." Her dolls celebrate the sisterhood of women.

Barbara Carleton Evans

124 Poli Street

Ventura, CA 93001

Phone: (805) 648-3860

Fax: (805) 643-5517

BarbEDolls@aol.com

Barbara's whimsical dolls have found their way into books, magazines, art shows, and stores. She enjoys designing doll forms using natural and found materials and often uses the materials at hand as her inspiration for designs.

Sue Eyet

Eyet & Co.

1827 Hopewell Road

Port Deposit, MD 21904

(410) 658-3462

Sue is a self-taught artist who works mainly with recycled materials and found objects to create one-of-a-kind angels, wind chimes, and folk-art signs, including the signage for the museum store for the American Visionary Art Museum.

Lorraine Gendron

P.O. Box 282

Hahnville, LA 70057

Phone: (985) 783-2173

Fax: (985) 783-1545

Lorraine is a Louisiana folk artist whose work reflects the culture and history of Louisiana.

Cindy Gorder

Cindy is a graphic designer and lifelong crafter living in rural Wisconsin.

Paula Grasdal

437 Trapelo Road

Belmont, MA 02478

Phone: (617) 489-4717

pgrasdal@netway.com

Paula is a printmaker and mixed-media artist living in the Boston area. Her work has appeared in several other Rockport publications including the Crafter's Project Book and Hand Lettering for Crafts.

Mary Ann Hall

220 Rockfish Orchard Drive

Afton, VA 22920

Phone: 540-456-6912

maryann@rockpub.com

Mary Ann loves making things and is an acquisitions editor with Rockport Publishers.

Heidi Harrison

4500 37th Street S., #211

St. Petersburg, FL 33711

Phone: (727) 867-4096

harrison69@juno.com

Heidi is a mother of three who enjoys a number of different crafts. Her work for Angel Crafts is her first foray into angel making.

Holly Harrison

391 Concord Avenue

Lexington, MA 02421

Phone: (781) 861-1192

hoha@mindspring.com

Along with being a crafter and writer, Holly is the editor of Angel Crafts.

Kelly A. Henderson

Chameleon Designs

998 N. 1100 W.

Farmington, UT 84025

Phone: (801) 451-7541

Kelly is a wife and the mother of four children, ages sixteen to one. A freelance designer and artist, she is the author of Charming Ribbonwork and has contributed to over a dozen craft and decorating books.

Mechtild H. Henry

P.O. Box 967

Kalaheo-Kauai, HI 96741

Phone: (808) 332-7065

Mechtild is married and lives in Hawaii. She enjoys sewing with her friends at a monthly "Kaffee Klatsch," making philodendron angels, and Hawaiian quilting.

Dawn Houser

www.dawnhouser.com

418 Laramie Drive

San Antonio, TX 78209

Phone: (210) 930-0373 Fax: (210) 930-0373

howzr@aol.com

dawn@dawnhouser.com

A full-time graphic designer and mother of three, Dawn creates sophisticated and charming images that she licenses to a variety of companies in different media as well as freelance designs for individuals and businesses.

Michelle Locke

4098 Leith Street

Burton, MI 48509

Phone: (810) 742-1726

Bigriglocke@aol.com

Michelle is married and has two children. She enjoys crafting as a hobby.

Sandra McCall

P.O. Box 4901

Covina, CA 91723

Phone and fax: (626) 967-6527

McCALLSS@aol.com

A freelance artist, Sandra enjoys finding new ways to marry basic art supplies and stamp-related products. Her interests include art bookbinding, surface embellishment, collage, and multimedia assemblage. Her book Making Gifts with Rubber Stamps is available in bookstores nationwide.

Laura McFadden

Laura McFadden Design, Inc.

49 Vinal Avenue

Somerville, MA 02143

Phone: (617) 625-7906

Fax: (617) 625-4040

laura.mcfadden@rcn.com

Laura is a freelance graphic designer and craftsperson.

Livia McRee

6028 W. Lindenhurst Avenue

Los Angeles, CA 90036

Phone: (323) 571-0092

Livia@liviamcree.com

Livia is a writer and designer. She is the author of three how-to craft books and has contributed to several others.

Neysa B. Neumann

4801 Osprey Drive S., Apt. 205

St. Petersburg, FL 33711

Phone: (727) 867-6339

neumannb@eckerd.edu

Neysa is an entrepreneur who studied with Ellen Simon in New York City. She has exhibited in New York, New Jersey, and Caracas, Venezuela. Her works are in Austria, Germany, Japan, and Venezuela, where she taught for the Association of Venezuelan/American women.

Angela M. Orrico

Prairie Primitives

1143 Wind Energy Pass

Batavia, IL 60510

Phone: (630) 222-3546

AngelaNCo@aol.com

www.prairie-primitives.com

Taking you back to times when things in life were simpler, Angela's Prairie Primitives capture the trendy rustic-country look. See more of her creations by visiting her web site.

Kathy Peterson

Kathy Peterson Productions Inc.

18709 S.E. River Ridge Road

Tequesta, FL 33469

Phone: (561) 744-2086

Fax: (561) 744-9199

Kathy@kathypeterson.com

www.kathypeterson.com

Kathy is a designer, author, and host of the national television show Town & Country Crafts with Kathy Peterson on GoodLife TV network. She has appeared on HGTV, Discovery Channel, and TNN. Her seven how-to videos include one devoted to angel crafts.

Elizabeth A. Philippi

11454 Clairmont Drive

Fenton, MI 48430

Phone: (810) 735-1361

LpEp825@aol.com

Elizabeth was introduced to crafting by her mother, who is a miniaturist. Her various interests include beadwork, cross-stitch, memory albums, and especially her sixteen-month-old daughter, Madison.

Anne Russell

8 Lester Terrace

Somerville, MA 02144

(617) 629-0769

arussell@erols.com

Anne designs jewelry and other accessories with a focus on polymer clay.

Judith Ann Snyder

From My Country Garden

200 Green Hills Road

Birdsboro, PA 19508

Phone: (610) 856-7236

Judith lives in Birdsboro, Pennsylvania, where she grows many of the plants used in the corn husk dolls and floral designs she makes for her business, From My Country Garden.

Kathy Underwood

4808 Adenmoor Avenue

Lakewood, CA 90713

Phone: (562) 429-6867 Fax: (562) 429-4348

rdu@webtv.net

Kathy has been a craft and doll pattern designer for the past fifteen years. You can view some of her designs at www.CraftsAntiques.com/vendors/ku-ku.htm.

Product Resource Guide

This guide is organized both by project and by vendor. Look under the project name to find out more about the particular products and materials used. For further information, or to purchase a product, consult the vendor listing that follows.

Close to Home

page 14 Dieter's Delight

- Nonrecycled metals available at Home Depot and hardware stores.
- Floral shears from Walmart.

page 16 Sugar Shell Angel

- Nonrecycled metals available at Home Depot and hardware stores.
- Floral shears from Walmart.
- #62 and #65 drill bits available at jewelry supply stores.
- Sterling silver wire from Terra Firma.

page 28 Rose Angel

- RIT fabric dyes for corn husks are Rose Pink #7, Kelly Green #32, and Taupe #34 for face and arms.
- 6" (15 cm) bleached and skeletonized leaves from craft stores or by mail order from Mountain Farms.
- Beautiful Braids Dark Blonde hair from Bolek's Craft Supplies, Inc.

In League with Nature

page 36 Maia, Springtime Angel

- BFK Rives paper is available at art supply stores.
- Windsor and Newton's Artisan Water-Mixable Oil Color is available at art supply stores.

page 40 Ayanna, Angel of Eternal Spring

- Paints are Dye-Na-Flow from Rupert Gibbon & Spider, Inc., in Bright Green, Violet, Sun Yellow, and Scarlet.
- Mod Podge available at craft stores.
- Pentel gel rollers available at stationery or stamp supply stores.

page 44 Crystal, Dewdrop Angel

- Jacquard Pearl-Ex pigment 651 in pearl white from Rupert Gibbon & Spider, Inc.
- Nonrecycled metals available at Home Depot and hardware stores.
- Floral shears from Walmart.

page 46 Summer Angel

- Aleene's Tacky Glue from craft stores.

page 48 Sun-Kissed Angel

- Fabri-Tac fabric glue by Beacon and Tacky Glue from Jo-Ann fabric stores and other craft stores.
- "Primitive Woman" rubber stamp (#GM4-GG) from Stamp Oasis.
- Permanent Ink Pen "Uniball Visions" from Office Depot.
- Fantastix paint sticks by Tsukineko from stamp stores or at Tsukineko.
- Fabrico stamp pads, Fabriko re-inkers from Tsukineko.

page 60 Winter Solstice Angel

- "Wireform" 1/8 pattern copper mesh available at art supply and craft stores.

Above the Horizon

page 64 Singing Angels

- Materials from Artistic Wire.

page 76 Friendship Angel

- Nonrecycled metals available at Home Depot and hardware stores.
- Floral shears from Walmart.
- #65 drill bit available at jewelry supply stores.
- Sterling silver wire from Terra Firma.

page 80 Angel of Good Fortune

- Milagros (Mexican miracle charms) can be found at www.buymexicanfolkart.com or on eBay.
- Shadow boxes from craft stores.

page 88 Blue Angel

- Recommended source: The Technique of Stained Glass by Patrick Reyntiens (Watson-Guptill Publishers, 1967).

Moments in Time

page 92 Kiah, Angel of New Beginnings

- Hot Foil pens available at Office Depot, Office Max, stationery or stamp supply stores.